DELICIOUS WAYS
TO CONTROL **DIABETES**

Family
Favorites

Cashew Chicken, page 123

Black Forest Trifle, page 49

DELICIOUS WAYS
TO CONTROL **DIABETES**

Family
Favorites

Oxmoor House®

Library of Congress Control Number: 2001-131174
ISBN: 0-8487-2490-9
Printed in the United States of America
First Printing 2001

Previously published as *Delicious Ways to Control Diabetes
Cookbook* © 1999 by Oxmoor House, Inc.

Be sure to check with your health-care provider
before making any changes in your diet.

Editor-in-Chief: Nancy Fitzpatrick Wyatt
Senior Foods Editor: Katherine M. Eakin
Senior Editor, Editorial Services: Olivia Kindig Wells
Art Director: James Boone

**Delicious Ways to Control Diabetes
Family Favorites**

Editor: Anne Chappell Cain, M.S., M.P.H., R.D.
Associate Art Director: Cynthia R. Cooper
Designer: Teresa Kent
Copy Editor: Jacqueline Giovanelli
Editorial Assistant: Heather Averett
Medical Advisors: David D. DeAtkine, Jr., M.D.;
     Kris Ernst, R.N., C.D.E.; Cathy A. Wesler, R.D.
Director, Test Kitchens: Kathleen Royal Phillips
Assistant Director, Test Kitchens: Gayle Hays Sadler
Test Kitchens Staff: Julie Christopher, Natalie E. King,
     Laurie Victoria Knowles, Rebecca W. Mohr,
     Jan A. Smith, Kate M. Wheeler, R.D.
Contributing Writer: Deborah Garrison Lowery
Senior Photographer: Jim Bathie
Photographer: Brit Huckabay
Additional photography: Ralph Anderson
Senior Photo Stylist: Kay E. Clarke
Photo Stylist: Virginia Cravens
Director, Production and Distribution: Phillip Lee
Associate Production Manager: James McDaniel
Production Assistant: Faye Porter Bonner

Cover: Chocolate Cheesecake, page 50

Contents

Introduction

Letter from the Editor 6

Update 7

Sugar Substitute Guide 10

Recipes

Appetizers & Beverages 11

Breads 25

Desserts 43

Fish & Shellfish 61

Meatless Main Dishes 79

Meats 95

Poultry 117

Salads 139

Sides 161

Soups & Sandwiches 181

7-Day Menu Planner 198

Nutrition Notes 200

Recipe Index 201

Metric Equivalents 207

Dear Friends,

To quote cookbook author Bert Green, "Food, like love, must never be a joyless experience." But for far too many people with diabetes, food has become not only joyless, but a source of confusion and stress. As a person who has lived with diabetes for over 27 years, I know that there is much to having diabetes that is not joy-filled. But I passionately believe that food does not have to be in that category. And as a dietitian, I have a personal goal to show you that it is possible to eat well and stay healthy.

The mission for *Family Favorites* is to help you enjoy wonderful food as you live with diabetes. There's no doubt: keeping your blood glucose under control will help prevent diabetes complications, and food

Eating well gives a spectacular joy to life.

ELSA SCHIAPARELLI, Italian fashion designer

plays a big part in this control. But no one ever said that the food had to taste bad!

Our staff of registered dietitians and cooking experts have put together over 100 recipes plus a one-week menu plan that will help you control your diabetes while you eat to your delight. Each recipe has nutrient information and exchanges, so you can work it into your meal plan whether you are counting carbohydrates or using exchange lists.

We realize that you don't have all day to spend in the kitchen—nor do you want to! So we have identified the quick recipes for you. We've also kept the ingredient lists simple by using items that you can find easily in your local grocery store. And we've filled the book with beautiful photographs so you can see exactly how the recipes will turn out.

Welcome, and please join me in the joy of good food.

Sincerely,

Anne Cain

Anne Cain, Editor

UPDATE

Good News for People with Diabetes

Until there's a cure, here's the best news we've heard recently for people with diabetes.

Inhalable Insulin on the Way

Don't hold your breath, but some relief from insulin injections may be on the market in three to five years. Two California companies — Inhale Therapeutic Systems (ITS) and Aradigm — have developed hand-held insulin inhalers. Each device is backed by a major pharmaceutical company and is currently being tested on patients.

A flashlight-sized device by ITS is in the final stage of Food and Drug Administration (FDA)-approved trials, but final FDA approval for marketing is still years away. The machine works on an air compression system and sprays a dry, powdered insulin.

Liquid aerosol insulin is dispensed through Aradigm's inhaler, which is the size of a portable radio. The rechargeable battery-powered inhaler will be able to record the date, time, and amount of actual doses received.

What are the advantages of inhalable insulin? It's easier to use, insulin can be stored for longer periods of time, and shot-shy people may be more likely to comply with insulin therapy if they don't have to inject themselves.

Note: Inhalable insulin may not be appropriate for everyone who uses insulin. Talk to your doctor about your treatment options, and be sure to look for more news about this revolutionary product.

Bottle Sleeves Prevent Insulin Mixups

INSULEEVES™ are color-coded for different types of insulin.

"I was horrified when I realized I had just injected my son with the wrong insulin," recalls Gail Hochman of Fairlawn, New Jersey. "I blamed it on the fact that the bottles look so much the same. Then I began hearing about other people who'd done the same thing, which potentially can be lethal."

Several years later, Hochman has come up with INSULEEVE™, a product that's ideal for preventing similar insulin mixups. The stretchy foam cover slips over the bottom of an insulin bottle and is labeled with a large letter indicating the type of insulin. The covers come in different colors, one color for each type of insulin.

"It helps older people with eyesight problems, too," says Hochman. "And it can prevent breakage if you accidentally drop the bottle on a tile floor."

Advocacy Hotline Opens

The new toll-free Diabetes Advocacy Hotline can be a direct line to help if you face discrimination at school or work, have questions about health-insurance coverage, or are interested in current or past legislation concerning diabetes.

The 24-hour hotline, sponsored by the American Diabetes Association (ADA), was launched in November 1998 with a grant from Parke-Davis. It can provide information about individual state legislation and can connect you directly to members of Congress. "It's one-stop shopping for diabetes advocacy information," says Joe LaMountain, ADA's National Director of Advocacy.

Call: 1-877-4-ADVOCC (1-877-423-8622)

No More Finger Pricks

Can you imagine placing a patch on your arm to find out your blood glucose level? If the FDA approves it, a non-invasive glucose monitor may be available soon after the year 2000.

Such a monitoring system has been developed by Technical Chemicals & Products, Inc. (Nasdaq: TCPI) and is in clinical trials now. Here's how it works:

A patch is placed on the skin for about five minutes, and the glucose under the skin is drawn into the patch. The glucose causes the patch to change color; the meter detects the color change and then provides a glucose reading.

For more information about this revolutionary monitoring system, check the company's website. **www.techchem.com**

- -

Healing Herbs?

"Take two cloves garlic and call me in the morning"? Everybody's talking about herbs and other natural remedies as ways to heal and treat diseases, including diabetes. Should you be listening? Maybe. Maybe not.

The claims about herbs are contradictory, and there is a lack of substantial research so it's hard to know if any herbs are effective in controlling diabetes.

It's hard to deny the claims of the people who swear that herbal treatments have improved their diabetes, and maybe they have. But the research is not conclusive.

A few herbs that are touted as treatments for diabetes-related conditions:

Bilberry ginkgo: improves circulation and prevents degenerative eye disease

Evening primrose oil: contains a type of fatty acid that helps with blood glucose regulation

Gymnema: lowers blood glucose

Siberian ginseng: helps reduce the effects of stress, therefore reducing blood glucose

Milk thistle: helps regenerate liver tissue

Garlic: helps reduce blood glucose

Fenugreek: helps lower blood glucose and improve cardiovascular system

The bottom line: proceed with caution. If you are taking herbal supplements, be sure to let your doctor know. If you're on insulin, don't take herbs instead of insulin. If you want to try herbs, talk to your doctor first because some herbs can be dangerous, especially if you take them with other medications. Watch for further developments in this ever-expanding area of health care.

Sugar Substitute Guide

Sugar substitutes used to be the only way people with diabetes could enjoy desserts and other sweet foods and still "follow the rules." Even though the sugar restriction has been relaxed, you may still choose to use sugar substitutes because they are "free" foods and you don't have to count them as carbohydrate.

There are a number of sugar substitutes on the market, and you may wonder which ones to use. It's really a matter of personal preference, but some sweeteners are better for cooking and baking than others. Below you'll find descriptions of sweeteners used in the Oxmoor House test kitchens.

Sugar Twin: low-calorie granulated sugar replacement containing saccharin.

- available in bulk, packets, and brown
- granulated form that can be measured like sugar
- some aftertaste because of the saccharin
- heat stable (can be used in cooking and baking)

Equal: a low-calorie sweetener containing Nutrasweet (aspartame).

- available as Equal Measure, Equal Spoonful, and Equal packets. Equal Measure is simply the bulk form of Equal packets; Equal Spoonful is granulated and can be measured in similar amounts to sugar.
- no bitter aftertaste
- prolonged exposure to high temperatures may reduce its sweetness
- appropriate for use in no-bake recipes or recipes that only have short cooking times

Sweet 'N Low: low-calorie sweetener containing saccharin.

- available in packets, bulk, brown, liquid, and tablets
- heat stable (can be used in cooking and baking)
- some aftertaste because of the saccharin

Appetizers & Beverages

Orange-Pineapple Slush, page 22

Speedy Salsa • Black Bean Dip • Orange Dip
Swiss-Onion Dip • Artichoke and Green Chile Dip • Pineapple
Cheese Ball • Pizza Bites • Mulled Cider Supreme
Raspberry Tea Spritzer • Orange-Pineapple Slush
Pink Tulip Punch • Mocha Punch

Ready in 1 Minute!

Speedy Salsa

Yield: 3 cups

1   (10-ounce) can diced tomatoes and green chiles, undrained
1   (14½-ounce) can no-salt-added stewed tomatoes, undrained
1   teaspoon pepper
1   clove garlic

Combine all ingredients in container of an electric blender; cover and process 30 seconds, stopping once to scrape down sides.

Serve with baked tortilla chips (chips not included in analysis).

Per Tablespoon:

Calories 3

Fat 0.0g (sat 0.0g)

Protein 0.1g

Carbohydrate 0.8g

Fiber 0.1g

Cholesterol 0mg

Sodium 21mg

Exchange: Free

Got a minute? Then you have time to make this spunky salsa. Four ingredients and a blender are all it takes.

Black Bean Dip

Yield: 2 cups

1   (15-ounce) can black beans, drained
1   (8-ounce) can no-salt-added tomato sauce
½   cup (2 ounces) shredded reduced-fat sharp Cheddar cheese
1   teaspoon chili powder

Combine beans and tomato sauce in a small saucepan; bring to a boil over medium heat, stirring occasionally. Remove from heat.

Mash beans with a potato masher or back of a spoon. Add cheese and chili powder; cook, stirring constantly, until cheese melts.

Serve dip warm with toasted pita chips or fresh vegetables (chips and vegetables not included in analysis).

Per Tablespoon:

Calories 19	Fiber 0.5g
Fat 0.4g (sat 0.2g)	Cholesterol 1mg
Protein 1.3g	Sodium 37mg
Carbohydrate 2.6g	Exchange: Free (up to 4 tablespoons)

If you're on a low-sodium diet, make this spicy dip with no-salt-added beans and serve it with unsalted chips or fresh vegetables.

Orange Dip

Yield: 1 cup

1   (8-ounce) carton vanilla low-fat yogurt
3   tablespoons tub-style light cream cheese, softened
1   (11-ounce) can mandarin oranges in light syrup, drained
      and chopped
1   teaspoon granulated sugar substitute (such as Sugar Twin)
2   teaspoons lime juice

Spoon yogurt onto several layers of heavy-duty paper towels, spreading to ½-inch thickness (Step 1). Cover with additional paper towels; let stand 5 minutes (Step 2).

Scrape yogurt into a bowl, using a rubber spatula (Step 3). Add cream cheese and remaining ingredients, stirring well until blended.

Serve with fresh fruit, such as apple or pear slices, strawberries, or pineapple chunks (fruit not included in analysis).

Per Tablespoon:

Calories 23	Fiber 0.0g
Fat 0.6g (sat 0.3g)	Cholesterol 2mg
Protein 0.9g	Sodium 22mg
Carbohydrate 3.6g	Exchange: Free (up to 3 tablespoons)

Making Yogurt Cheese

Step 1   Step 2   Step 3

Swiss-Onion Dip

Yield: 2¼ cups

1   (10-ounce) package frozen chopped onion, thawed
2   cups (8 ounces) shredded reduced-fat Swiss cheese
1   cup nonfat mayonnaise
1   tablespoon coarse-grained Dijon mustard
⅛   teaspoon pepper

Drain onion on paper towels.

Combine onion and remaining ingredients in a 1-quart baking dish.

Bake at 325° for 25 minutes or until bubbly and lightly browned.

Serve with low-fat crackers (crackers not included in analysis).

Per Tablespoon:

Calories 28	Fiber 0.0g
Fat 1.1g (sat 0.6g)	Cholesterol 4mg
Protein 2.3g	Sodium 103mg
Carbohydrate 2.1g	Exchange: Free (up to 3 tablespoons)

Artichoke and Green Chile Dip

Yield: 2¾ cups

⅔ cup nonfat mayonnaise
½ cup plain low-fat yogurt
1 (14-ounce) can artichoke hearts, drained and chopped
1 (4-ounce) can chopped green chiles, drained
½ cup freshly grated Parmesan cheese, divided
¼ teaspoon garlic powder
¼ teaspoon hot sauce
Cooking spray
Fresh green chile slices (optional)

Combine mayonnaise and yogurt in a medium bowl, stirring until smooth. Add artichoke, chopped chiles, 6 tablespoons Parmesan cheese, garlic powder, and hot sauce, stirring well.

Spoon mixture into a 1-quart baking dish coated with cooking spray. Bake, uncovered, at 350° for 25 minutes.

Sprinkle with remaining 2 tablespoons Parmesan cheese. Turn oven temperature to broil, and cook 1½ minutes or until lightly browned.

Garnish with green chile slices, if desired. Serve with Melba toast rounds or breadsticks (rounds and breadsticks not included in analysis).

Per Tablespoon:

Calories 13	Fiber 0.1g
Fat 0.4g (sat 0.2g)	Cholesterol 1mg
Protein 0.7g	Sodium 78mg
Carbohydrate 1.7g	Exchange: Free (up to 4 tablespoons)

Pineapple Cheese Ball

Yield: 2¼ cups

¾ cup (3 ounces) shredded fat-free sharp Cheddar cheese
½ cup finely chopped green pepper
2 teaspoons grated onion
1 (8-ounce) can crushed pineapple in juice, well drained
½ (8-ounce) package ⅓-less-fat cream cheese (Neufchâtel), softened
½ (8-ounce) package fat-free cream cheese, softened
⅔ cup chopped fresh parsley

Combine first 6 ingredients in a medium bowl. Cover and chill 30 minutes.

Shape cheese mixture into a ball; roll in chopped parsley, coating thoroughly. Cover and chill at least 3 hours.

Serve with Melba toast rounds or low-fat crackers (rounds and crackers not included in analysis).

Per Tablespoon:

Calories 17	Fiber 0.1g
Fat 0.8g (sat 0.5g)	Cholesterol 3mg
Protein 1.6g	Sodium 49mg
Carbohydrate 0.9g	Exchange: Free (up to 4 tablespoons)

We tested this cheese ball using only fat-free cream cheese, but found that a combination of fat-free and reduced-fat cream cheese produced a creamier dip.

Pizza Bites

Yield: 2 dozen appetizers

¾ cup (3 ounces) shredded part-skim mozzarella cheese
⅓ cup freshly grated Parmesan cheese
1 (14-ounce) package mini English muffins
⅓ cup chopped Canadian bacon
⅓ cup chopped green pepper

Combine mozzarella and Parmesan cheeses; set aside.

Cut each muffin in half horizontally and place on an ungreased baking sheet. Sprinkle bacon, green pepper, and cheese mixture evenly on muffin halves.

Bake at 400° for 10 to 12 minutes or until lightly browned.

Serve warm.

Per Appetizer:

Calories 56	Fiber 0.0g
Fat 1.2g (sat 0.7g)	Cholesterol 5mg
Protein 3.5g	Sodium 147mg
Carbohydrate 7.8g	Exchanges: ½ Starch, ½ Lean Meat

Mulled Cider Supreme

Yield: 5 (1-cup) servings

4½	cups unsweetened apple cider
1	cup water
2	tablespoons granulated brown sugar substitute (such as brown Sugar Twin)
2	(3-inch) sticks cinnamon
5	whole cloves
3	whole allspice
1	(2-inch) piece peeled gingerroot

Combine first 3 ingredients in a saucepan, stirring well.

Place cinnamon sticks and remaining 3 ingredients on a 6-inch square of cheesecloth (Step 1); tie with string (Step 2). Add spice bag to cider mixture.

Bring to a simmer over medium-high heat, stirring occasionally. Reduce heat to low; cook, uncovered, 15 minutes, stirring occasionally. Discard spice bag. Pour into individual mugs, and serve warm.

Per Serving:

Calories 109
Fat 0.2g (sat 0.0g)
Protein 0.1g
Carbohydrate 27.1g

Fiber 0.4g
Cholesterol 0mg
Sodium 13mg
Exchanges: 2 Fruit

Tie a Spice Bundle

Step 1

Step 2

Raspberry Tea Spritzer

Yield: 4 (1-cup) servings

2   cups boiling water
4   raspberry zinger herb tea bags
2   cups sugar-free ginger ale, chilled

Pour boiling water over tea bags; cover and steep 5 minutes.

Remove tea bags from water, squeezing gently; let tea cool. Stir in chilled ginger ale.

Serve over ice.

Per Serving:

Calories 2	**Fiber** 0.0g
Fat 0.0g (sat 0.0g)	**Cholesterol** 0mg
Protein 0.0g	**Sodium** 22mg
Carbohydrate 0.5g	**Exchange:** Free

You can make this refreshing sparkling tea with any flavored tea bags. And since one serving has less than 1 gram of carbohydrate, you don't have to count it in your meal plan.

Orange-Pineapple Slush

Yield: 4 (1-cup) servings

3	cups ice cubes
1	cup orange juice
½	cup pineapple juice
¼	cup lemon juice
3	tablespoons granulated sugar substitute (such as Sugar Twin)

Combine all ingredients in container of an electric blender or food processor; cover and process on high speed until smooth and frothy.

Serve immediately.

Per Serving:

Calories 57	Fiber 0.2g
Fat 0.1g (sat 0.0g)	Cholesterol 0mg
Protein 0.6g	Sodium 13mg
Carbohydrate 14.3g	Exchange: 1 Fruit

(Photograph on page 11)

Pink Tulip Punch

Yield: 12 (1-cup) servings

1   (12-ounce) package frozen unsweetened raspberries, thawed
2   medium-size ripe bananas, peeled and sliced
2   (12-ounce) cans frozen orange-pineapple-apple juice
       concentrate, thawed
2   cups water
1   (32-ounce) bottle berry-flavored sparkling mineral water, chilled

Place raspberries in container of an electric blender; cover and process until smooth. Pour raspberry puree through a wire-mesh strainer into a bowl, discarding pulp and seeds remaining in strainer. Return strained puree to blender container. Add sliced banana and 1 can juice concentrate; cover and process until smooth.

Pour mixture into a large freezer-proof container. Stir in remaining 1 can juice concentrate and 2 cups water. Cover and freeze 4 hours or until slushy.

To serve, transfer juice mixture to a small punch bowl. Stir in mineral water, and serve immediately.

Per Serving:

Calories 122	Fiber 3.2g
Fat 0.4g (sat 0.0g)	Cholesterol 0mg
Protein 1.8g	Sodium 18mg
Carbohydrate 29.4g	Exchanges: 2 Fruit

Mocha Punch

Yield: 40 (1-cup) servings

1   (2-ounce) jar instant coffee granules
1   cup boiling water
¾   cup granulated sugar substitute (such as Sugar Twin)
1   gallon fat-free milk
½   gallon chocolate no-sugar-added, reduced-fat ice cream, softened
½   gallon vanilla no-sugar-added, fat-free ice cream, softened
1   cup frozen fat-free whipped topping, thawed

Combine coffee granules and boiling water, stirring until coffee granules dissolve. Add sugar substitute, stirring until dissolved. Cover and chill.

Combine coffee mixture and milk in a large punch bowl; gently stir in ice creams. Spoon whipped topping onto ice cream mixture.

Serve immediately.

Per Serving:

Calories 124	Fiber 0.0g
Fat 0.2g (sat 0.1g)	Cholesterol 2mg
Protein 7.5g	Sodium 124mg
Carbohydrate 23.5g	Exchanges: 1 Skim Milk, 1 Carbohydrate

No one will ever suspect that this sweet, creamy punch is a diabetic recipe.

Breads

Banana Bread, page 40

Cinnamon French Toast • Cheesy French Bread • Cheddar
Drop Biscuits • Italian Biscuit Knots • Scones • Yogurt-Pecan
Waffles • Blueberry Muffins • Applesauce-Bran Muffins
Carrot-Pineapple-Bran Muffins • Chile-Cheese Cornbread
Cumin Quick Bread • Banana Bread • Spiced Pumpkin Bread
Caraway-Swiss Casserole Bread

Cinnamon French Toast

Yield: 4 servings

½   cup fat-free egg substitute
½   cup fat-free milk
½   to ¾ teaspoon ground cinnamon
Cooking spray
1   tablespoon plus 1 teaspoon reduced-calorie margarine, divided
4   (1⅓-ounce) slices whole wheat bread

Combine first 3 ingredients in a shallow bowl, stirring well with a wire whisk.

Coat a nonstick skillet with cooking spray. Add 1 teaspoon margarine; place over medium heat until margarine melts.

Dip 1 bread slice into egg substitute mixture. Place coated bread in skillet; cook until browned and crisp on each side, turning once. Repeat procedure with remaining margarine, bread, and egg substitute mixture.

Serve immediately.

Per Serving:

Calories 141	Fiber 3.1g
Fat 4.4g (sat 0.4g)	Cholesterol 1mg
Protein 7.1g	Sodium 248mg
Carbohydrate 21.2g	Exchanges: 1½ Starch, 1 Fat

Cheesy French Bread

Yield: 16 servings

1½   cups (6 ounces) shredded reduced-fat Monterey Jack cheese
½   cup reduced-fat mayonnaise
1½   teaspoons dried parsley flakes
⅛   teaspoon garlic powder
1   (16-ounce) loaf French bread, cut in half horizontally

Combine first 4 ingredients. Spread on cut sides of bread; place on a baking sheet.

Bake at 350° for 10 to 15 minutes or until cheese is melted.

Slice into serving size pieces, and serve warm.

Per Serving:

Calories 134	Fiber 0.6g
Fat 4.6g (sat 1.7g)	Cholesterol 10mg
Protein 5.8g	Sodium 288mg
Carbohydrate 16.4g	Exchanges: 1 Starch, ½ High-Fat Meat

Cheddar Drop Biscuits

Yield: 1 dozen

2	cups reduced-fat biscuit and baking mix (such as Bisquick)
½	cup (2 ounces) shredded reduced-fat sharp Cheddar cheese
¾	cup fat-free milk
Cooking spray	
2	tablespoons reduced-calorie margarine, melted
¼	teaspoon garlic powder
½	teaspoon dried parsley flakes, crushed

Combine baking mix and cheese in a bowl; make a well in center of mixture. Add milk, stirring just until dry ingredients are moistened.

Drop dough by rounded tablespoonfuls, 2 inches apart, onto a baking sheet coated with cooking spray. Bake at 450° for 8 to 10 minutes or until biscuits are golden.

Combine margarine, garlic powder, and parsley flakes; brush over warm biscuits, and serve immediately.

Per Biscuit:

Calories 106	Fiber 0.3g
Fat 3.5g (sat 1.0g)	Cholesterol 3mg
Protein 3.4g	Sodium 291mg
Carbohydrate 15.0g	Exchanges: 1 Starch, ½ Fat

Reduced-fat biscuit and baking mix is a handy item to keep in your pantry so that you can always whip up "homemade" biscuits for supper.

Italian Biscuit Knots

Yield: 1 dozen

2   cups plus 2 tablespoons reduced-fat biscuit and baking mix
        (such as Bisquick), divided
1½   teaspoons dried Italian seasoning
¾   cup fat-free milk
1   tablespoon fat-free Italian dressing

Combine 2 cups baking mix and Italian seasoning, stirring well.
Add milk; stir with a fork just until dry ingredients are moistened.

Sprinkle remaining 2 tablespoons baking mix evenly over work
surface. Turn dough out onto floured surface. Divide dough into
12 equal portions. (Dough will be very soft.) Roll each portion of
dough into an 8-inch rope (Step 1); tie each rope into a loose knot
(Step 2). Place knots on a baking sheet. Brush Italian dressing
evenly over biscuits. Bake at 400° for 12 minutes or until golden.

Serve warm.

Per Biscuit:

Calories 87	Fiber 0.3g
Fat 1.4g (sat 0.3g)	Cholesterol 0mg
Protein 2.2g	Sodium 267mg
Carbohydrate 16.1g	Exchange: 1 Starch

Making Biscuit Knots

Step 1

Step 2

Scones

Yield: 1 dozen

1½ cups all-purpose flour
2 teaspoons baking powder
½ teaspoon baking soda
3 tablespoons margarine
⅓ cup nonfat buttermilk
3 tablespoons brown sugar
1 teaspoon vanilla extract
1 egg, lightly beaten

Combine first 3 ingredients in a medium bowl; cut in margarine with a pastry blender until mixture resembles coarse meal.

Combine buttermilk and remaining 3 ingredients in a medium bowl, stirring well with a wire whisk. Add buttermilk mixture to flour mixture, stirring just until dry ingredients are moistened.

Turn dough out onto a lightly floured surface, and knead lightly for 30 seconds. Divide dough in half, and pat each half into a ¾-inch-thick circle. Cut each circle into 6 wedges. Place wedges on an ungreased baking sheet. Bake at 400° for 15 to 18 minutes or until lightly browned. Serve warm.

Per Wedge:

Calories 106	Fiber 0.4g
Fat 3.0g (sat 1.0g)	Cholesterol 18mg
Protein 2.0g	Sodium 181mg
Carbohydrate 16.0g	Exchanges: 1 Starch, ½ Fat

Brown sugar helps make these scones tender as well as sweet. Even with real sugar, each wedge has only 16 grams of carbohydrate.

Yogurt-Pecan Waffles

Yield: 8 (4-inch) waffles

1	cup all-purpose flour
1	teaspoon baking powder
½	teaspoon baking soda
¼	teaspoon salt
1	cup plus 2 tablespoons plain nonfat yogurt
¼	cup fat-free egg substitute
2	tablespoons reduced-calorie margarine, melted
2	tablespoons finely chopped pecans, toasted

Cooking spray
Sugar-free maple syrup (optional)

Combine first 4 ingredients in a medium bowl. Combine yogurt, egg substitute, and margarine; add to dry ingredients, beating well at medium speed of an electric mixer. Stir in pecans.

Coat an 8-inch waffle iron with cooking spray; allow waffle iron to preheat. For each waffle, pour 1 cup batter onto hot waffle iron, spreading batter to edges. Bake 4 to 5 minutes or until steaming stops. Cut each waffle into 4 squares.

Serve with sugar-free syrup, if desired.

Per Waffle:

Calories 112	Fiber 0.6g
Fat 3.9g (sat 0.2g)	Cholesterol 1mg
Protein 4.4g	Sodium 215mg
Carbohydrate 15.1g	Exchanges: 1 Starch, 1 Fat

Blueberry Muffins

Yield: 1 dozen

1¾ cups all-purpose flour
3 tablespoons sugar
3 tablespoons granulated sugar substitute (such as Sugar Twin)
2 teaspoons baking powder
¼ teaspoon salt
½ teaspoon ground allspice
1 cup fresh or frozen blueberries, thawed and drained
¾ cup fat-free milk
¼ cup vegetable oil
1 egg, lightly beaten
1 teaspoon grated lemon rind
1 teaspoon grated orange rind
1 teaspoon vanilla extract
Cooking spray

Combine first 6 ingredients in a medium bowl; add blueberries, and toss to coat. Make a well in center of flour mixture. Combine milk and next 5 ingredients; add to flour mixture, stirring just until dry ingredients are moistened.

Spoon batter into muffin pans coated with cooking spray, filling two-thirds full. Bake at 400° for 20 to 25 minutes or until golden. Remove muffins from pans immediately, and cool on wire racks.

Per Muffin:

Calories 142	**Fiber** 1.1g
Fat 5.5g (sat 1.0g)	**Cholesterol** 19mg
Protein 3.0g	**Sodium** 145mg
Carbohydrate 20.3g	**Exchanges:** 1 Starch, ½ Fruit, 1 Fat

In L.A., everybody sends everybody muffins, as a little gesture of good will, like a thank-you muffin or a get-well muffin or a welcome-to-the-show muffin....

JANEANE GAROFALO, *actress*

Applesauce-Bran Muffins

Yield: 2 dozen

2½ cups all-purpose flour
¼   cup sugar
¼   cup granulated sugar substitute (such as Sugar Twin)
1½ teaspoons baking soda
½   teaspoon salt
2   cups nonfat buttermilk
¼   cup fat-free milk
½   cup fat-free egg substitute
½   cup unsweetened applesauce
3   cups unprocessed wheat bran
Cooking spray

Combine first 5 ingredients in a large bowl. Make a well in center of mixture, and set aside. Combine buttermilk and next 3 ingredients, stirring well with a wire whisk. Stir in bran; let stand 5 minutes.

Add bran mixture to flour mixture, stirring just until dry ingredients are moistened.

Spoon batter evenly into muffin pans coated with cooking spray, filling three-fourths full. Bake at 400° for 22 to 24 minutes or until golden. Remove muffins from pans immediately, and cool on wire racks.

Per Muffin:

Calories 88	Fiber 3.6g
Fat 0.7g (sat 0.1g)	Cholesterol 1mg
Protein 3.8g	Sodium 158mg
Carbohydrate 18.9g	Exchange: 1 Starch

Carrot-Pineapple-Bran Muffins

Yield: 18 muffins

1¾ cups all-purpose flour
¼ cup sugar
1 teaspoon baking powder
1 teaspoon baking soda
1 teaspoon ground cinnamon
¾ cup fat-free milk
1 egg, lightly beaten
1 (8-ounce) can crushed pineapple in juice, undrained
2 tablespoons margarine, melted
1 cup wheat bran flakes cereal
1 cup shredded carrot
2 tablespoons water
Cooking spray

Combine first 5 ingredients in a large bowl. Make a well in center of mixture, and set aside. Combine milk and next 3 ingredients, stirring well. Stir in cereal; let stand 5 minutes.

Place carrot and water in a small saucepan. Cover and bring to a boil; reduce heat, and cook 1 to 2 minutes or until carrot is tender. Drain and set aside.

Add cereal mixture to flour mixture; add carrot, and stir just until dry ingredients are moistened. Spoon batter evenly into muffin pans coated with cooking spray, filling two-thirds full. Bake at 350° for 20 to 22 minutes or until golden. Remove muffins from pans immediately, and cool on wire racks.

Per Muffin:

Calories 88	Fiber 0.7g
Fat 1.9g (sat 0.4g)	Cholesterol 12mg
Protein 2.1g	Sodium 109mg
Carbohydrate 15.8g	Exchange: 1 Starch

Chile-Cheese Cornbread

Yield: 16 servings

1   cup yellow cornmeal
1   cup all-purpose flour
1   tablespoon plus 1 teaspoon baking powder
¼   teaspoon salt
¼   cup nonfat dry milk powder
1   tablespoon granulated sugar substitute (such as Sugar Twin)
1   cup water
½   cup fat-free egg substitute
2   tablespoons vegetable oil
¾   cup (3 ounces) shredded reduced-fat Cheddar cheese
1   (4-ounce) can chopped green chiles, drained
Cooking spray

Combine first 6 ingredients in a medium bowl; make a well in center of mixture. Combine water, egg substitute, and oil; add to flour mixture, stirring just until dry ingredients are moistened. Stir in cheese and green chiles.

Pour batter into an 8-inch square baking dish coated with cooking spray. Bake at 375° for 30 minutes or until golden.

Cut into squares, and serve warm.

Per Serving:

Calories 105	**Fiber** 0.7g
Fat 3.0g (sat 0.9g)	**Cholesterol** 4mg
Protein 4.6g	**Sodium** 227mg
Carbohydrate 14.7g	**Exchanges:** 1 Starch, ½ Fat

Cumin Quick Bread

Yield: 10 (¾-inch) slices

1½ cups all-purpose flour
2 tablespoons granulated sugar substitute (such as Sugar Twin)
1 tablespoon baking powder
2 teaspoons ground cumin
½ teaspoon cumin seed, slightly crushed
¼ teaspoon dry mustard
¼ teaspoon salt
⅔ cup fat-free milk
⅓ cup fat-free egg substitute
2½ tablespoons vegetable oil
2 tablespoons picante sauce
Cooking spray

Combine first 7 ingredients in a medium bowl; make a well in center of mixture. Combine milk and next 3 ingredients; stir well. Add to flour mixture, stirring just until dry ingredients are moistened.

Spoon batter into a 8½- x 4½- x 3-inch loafpan coated with cooking spray. Bake at 350° for 40 minutes or until a wooden pick inserted in center comes out clean. Remove from pan, and let cool on a wire rack.

Per Slice:

Calories 115	Fiber 0.6g
Fat 3.9g (sat 0.5g)	Cholesterol 0mg
Protein 3.4g	Sodium 262mg
Carbohydrate 16.4g	Exchanges: 1 Starch, 1 Fat

Cumin is a nutty, aromatic spice that is one of the ingredients in curry and chili powders. This savory cumin bread is great with spicy dishes like chili or hearty bean soup.

Banana Bread

Yield: 16 (½-inch) slices

¾   cup all-purpose flour
¾   cup whole wheat flour
1   teaspoon baking powder
1   teaspoon baking soda
¼   cup sugar
2   tablespoons margarine, melted
4   medium-size ripe bananas, peeled and mashed
1   egg, lightly beaten
Cooking spray

Combine first 4 ingredients in a large bowl. Combine sugar and next 3 ingredients; add to flour mixture, stirring just until dry ingredients are moistened.

Pour batter into an 8½- x 4½- x 3-inch loafpan coated with cooking spray. Bake at 350° for 50 minutes or until a wooden pick inserted in center comes out clean. Cool in pan on a wire rack 10 minutes; remove from pan, and let cool completely on wire rack.

Per Slice:

Calories 96	**Fiber** 1.7g
Fat 2.1g (sat 0.5g)	**Cholesterol** 13mg
Protein 2.0g	**Sodium** 93mg
Carbohydrate 18.4g	**Exchange:** 1 Starch

(Photograph on page 25)

This staff favorite is an ideal way to use bananas that are too ripe to peel and eat. Four bananas make the bread extrasweet.

Spiced Pumpkin Bread

Yield: 18 (½-inch) slices

2	cups sifted cake flour
2	teaspoons baking powder
¼	teaspoon baking soda
¼	teaspoon salt
½	cup firmly packed brown sugar
1	teaspoon ground cinnamon
¼	teaspoon ground ginger
¼	teaspoon ground cloves
1	cup canned pumpkin
¼	cup unsweetened applesauce
3	tablespoons vegetable oil
2	eggs, lightly beaten
1	teaspoon vanilla extract

Cooking spray

Combine first 8 ingredients in a medium bowl; make a well in center of mixture. Combine pumpkin and next 4 ingredients; add to flour mixture, stirring just until dry ingredients are moistened.

Spoon batter into a 9- x 5- x 3-inch loafpan coated with cooking spray. Bake at 350° for 45 to 50 minutes or until a wooden pick inserted in center comes out clean. Cool in pan on a wire rack 10 minutes; remove loaf from pan, and let cool completely on wire rack.

Per Slice:

Calories 103	Fiber 1.0g
Fat 3.0g (sat 0.6g)	Cholesterol 25mg
Protein 1.9g	Sodium 115mg
Carbohydrate 17.2g	Exchanges: 1 Starch, ½ Fat

Caraway-Swiss Casserole Bread

Yield: 14 servings

1 (16-ounce) package hot roll mix
1⅓ cups warm water (105° to 115°)
1 cup (4 ounces) shredded reduced-fat Swiss cheese
¼ cup finely chopped onion
2 tablespoons margarine, melted
1 tablespoon caraway seeds
1 teaspoon cracked pepper
Cooking spray

Combine yeast packet from roll mix and warm water in a large bowl. Let stand 5 minutes. Add three-fourths of flour packet from roll mix, cheese, and next 4 ingredients. Beat at low speed of an electric mixer until blended. Stir in remaining flour from roll mix.

Scrape dough from sides of bowl. Cover and let rise in a warm place (85°), free from drafts, 30 minutes or until doubled in bulk. Stir dough 25 strokes.

Spoon dough into a 2-quart casserole dish coated with cooking spray. Bake at 350° for 45 to 50 minutes or until loaf is browned and sounds hollow when tapped.

Cut into wedges, and serve warm.

Per Wedge:

Calories 160	Fiber 0.7g
Fat 4.4g (sat 1.1g)	Cholesterol 5mg
Protein 6.1g	Sodium 246mg
Carbohydrate 23.1g	Exchanges: 1½ Starch, 1 Fat

Desserts

Chocolate-Peppermint Ice Cream Cake, page 60

Spiced Bananas • Orange-Pumpkin Tarts • Strawberry Tarts
Chocolate Cereal Bars • Black Forest Trifle • Chocolate Cheesecake
Chocolate Ice Cream • Fudgy Peanut Butter Ice Cream
Homemade Peach Ice Cream • Frozen Pineapple Yogurt with
Raspberries • Ice Cream Sandwich Dessert • Cookies 'n Cream
Crunch • Chocolate-Peppermint Ice Cream Cake

Spiced Bananas

Yield: 4 servings

Butter-flavored cooking spray
3   tablespoons reduced-calorie margarine
3   tablespoons granulated brown sugar substitute (such as brown
        Sugar Twin)
½   teaspoon vanilla extract
Dash of ground cinnamon
2   very ripe bananas, split lengthwise
2   cups vanilla no-sugar-added, fat-free ice cream

Coat a medium nonstick skillet with cooking spray; add margarine, and place over medium heat until margarine melts. Add brown sugar substitute, vanilla, and cinnamon; cook 1 minute or until sugar substitute dissolves.

Arrange banana in skillet; cook over medium-high heat 2 minutes or until thoroughly heated, turning once.

To serve, spoon banana mixture evenly over ½-cup portions of ice cream.

Per Serving:

Calories 200	**Fiber** 1.7g
Fat 5.8g (sat 0.9g)	**Cholesterol** 0mg
Protein 4.6g	**Sodium** 165mg
Carbohydrate 37.9g	**Exchanges:** 1½ Starch, 1 Fruit, 1 Fat

Orange-Pumpkin Tarts

Yield: 4 servings

1	cup crumbled sugar-free oatmeal cookies (5 cookies)
2	tablespoons reduced-calorie margarine, melted
Cooking spray	
1	teaspoon all-purpose flour
½	cup canned pumpkin
½	cup evaporated fat-free milk
¼	cup granulated sugar substitute (such as Sugar Twin)
¼	cup fat-free egg substitute
2	tablespoons orange juice
½	teaspoon pumpkin pie spice
¼	cup frozen reduced-calorie whipped topping, thawed

Combine cookie crumbs and margarine, stirring well. Coat 4 (4-inch) tartlet pans with cooking spray. Sprinkle flour evenly over bottoms of pans. Press crumb mixture into bottoms and three-fourths way up sides of pans. Bake at 375° for 5 minutes.

Combine pumpkin and next 5 ingredients, stirring well with a wire whisk. Pour evenly into prepared crusts.

Bake at 375° for 25 minutes or until set. Let cool completely on a wire rack.

To serve, top each tart with 1 tablespoon whipped topping.

Per Serving:

Calories 234	Fiber 1.3g
Fat 10.9g (sat 2.2g)	Cholesterol 1mg
Protein 5.8g	Sodium 213mg
Carbohydrate 30.0g	Exchanges: 2 Starch, 2 Fat

A tribute to the strawberry—"Doubtless God could have made a better berry, but doubtless God never did."

WILLIAM BUTLER, 16th-century author

Strawberry Tarts

Yield: 4 servings

⅓ cup vanilla low-fat yogurt sweetened with aspartame
1 cup graham cracker crumbs (8 crackers)
⅛ teaspoon ground cinnamon
3 tablespoons reduced-calorie margarine, melted
Cooking spray
⅓ cup fat-free cream cheese, softened
2 teaspoons granulated sugar substitute with aspartame (such as Equal Spoonful)
1 teaspoon vanilla extract
1 cup sliced fresh strawberries
1 tablespoon low-sugar apple jelly, melted
Fresh mint sprigs (optional)

Spread yogurt onto several layers of paper towels; cover with additional paper towels, and let stand 10 minutes.

Combine graham cracker crumbs, cinnamon, and margarine, stirring well. Press crumb mixture evenly into 4 (4-inch) tartlet pans coated with cooking spray. Bake at 350° for 8 minutes; remove from oven, and let cool.

Combine drained yogurt, cream cheese, sugar substitute, and vanilla, stirring well. Spoon mixture evenly into prepared crusts. Cover and chill at least 3 hours. To serve, arrange strawberries evenly over yogurt mixture; brush with jelly. Garnish with mint sprigs, if desired.

Per Serving:

Calories 204	Fiber 1.0g
Fat 8.5g (sat 0.9g)	Cholesterol 5mg
Protein 5.4g	Sodium 380mg
Carbohydrate 26.3g	Exchanges: 1½ Starch, 2 Fat

Chocolate Cereal Bars

Yield: 18 bars (serving size: 1 bar)

3   tablespoons margarine
¼   cup granulated brown sugar substitute (such as brown Sugar Twin)
2   cups miniature marshmallows
4   cups crispy rice cereal
2   cups whole wheat flake cereal
Cooking spray
1   (5¼-ounce) package sugar-free chocolate whipped frosting mix
       (such as Sweet 'N Low)

Melt margarine in a large saucepan over medium heat. Add sugar substitute; stir well. Add marshmallows; cook, stirring constantly, until marshmallows melt. Remove from heat; stir in cereals.

Press cereal mixture evenly into bottom of a 13- x 9- x 2-inch pan coated with cooking spray. Let cool at least 1 hour.

Prepare chocolate frosting mix according to package directions. Spread frosting over cereal mixture. Cover and chill 8 hours or until frosting is slightly firm. Cut into 3- x 2-inch bars.

Per Bar:

Calories 109	Fiber 0.3g
Fat 4.7g (sat 1.4g)	Cholesterol 0mg
Protein 1.5g	Sodium 123mg
Carbohydrate 16.9g	Exchanges: 1 Starch, 1 Fat

Black Forest Trifle

Yield: 12 servings

1   (8-ounce) package chocolate sugar-free, low-fat cake mix
          (such as Sweet 'N Low)
¾   cup water
1   (1-ounce) box chocolate sugar-free, fat-free instant pudding mix
2   cups fat-free milk
1   (16-ounce) package frozen no-sugar-added pitted cherries
2   or 3 drops red food coloring
2   cups fat-free frozen whipped topping, thawed
Sugar-free chocolate curls (optional)

Prepare cake mix according to package directions, using ¾ cup water. Let cake cool in pan; remove from pan, cut into cubes.

Prepare pudding mix according to package directions, using 2 cups fat-free milk; chill at least 30 minutes.

Thaw cherries, reserving ¼ cup juice. Combine cherries, juice, and food coloring.

Place half of cake cubes in a 3-quart trifle bowl; Spoon half of cherries over cake; spread 1 cup pudding over cherries, and top with half of whipped topping. Repeat layers. Top with chocolate curls. Cover and chill at least 8 hours.

Per Serving:

Calories 132	Fiber 0.9g
Fat 1.7g (sat 0.6g)	Cholesterol 1mg
Protein 3.3g	Sodium 151mg
Carbohydrate 28.1g	Exchanges: 1 Starch, 1 Fruit

Chocolate Cheesecake

Yield: 12 servings

1	(5.25-ounce) package sugar-free chocolate graham crackers, crushed
⅓	cup reduced-calorie margarine, melted
¼	teaspoon ground cinnamon
	Cooking spray
1	envelope unflavored gelatin
1	cup fat-free milk
2½	(8-ounce) packages ⅓-less-fat cream cheese (Neufchâtel), softened
2	teaspoons vanilla extract
¾	cup plus 2 tablespoons granulated sugar substitute with aspartame (such as Equal Spoonful)
¼	cup unsweetened cocoa
5	(0.6-ounce) sugar-free chocolate wafer bars, coarsely chopped (such as Sweet 'N Low)

Combine first 3 ingredients, stirring well. Press into bottom and 1 inch up sides of a 9-inch springform pan coated with cooking spray. Bake at 350° for 8 minutes. Remove from oven; let cool on a wire rack.

Sprinkle gelatin over milk in a small saucepan; let stand 1 minute. Cook over low heat, stirring until gelatin dissolves, about 2 minutes. Let cool slightly.

Beat cream cheese at medium speed of an electric mixer until creamy. Add vanilla, beating well. Add gelatin mixture, beating until smooth. Add sugar substitute and cocoa; beat just until blended. Pour mixture into prepared crust. Cover and chill at least 3 hours or until set. Before serving, top with chopped wafers.

Per Serving:

Calories 238	Fiber 1.5g
Fat 16.5g (sat 8.4g)	Cholesterol 36mg
Protein 8.1g	Sodium 308mg
Carbohydrate 20.8g	Exchanges: 1½ Starch, 3 Fat

My favorite word is "chocolate."
It's the most delicious word I know...
The word — if I read it or write it
or say it — tastes just great to me.

MAIDA HEATTER, American food writer

chocolate

Chocolate Ice Cream

Yield: 8 (½-cup) servings

2	envelopes unflavored gelatin
4	cups evaporated fat-free milk, divided
¾	cup fat-free egg substitute
1	tablespoon vanilla extract
⅓	cup unsweetened cocoa
7¼	teaspoons or 24 packets sugar substitute with aspartame (such as Equal Measure or Equal packets)
1	(2.8-ounce) sugar-free milk chocolate bar, chopped

Sprinkle gelatin over 2 cups evaporated milk in a medium saucepan; let stand 5 minutes. Cook over medium heat until gelatin dissolves and mixture just comes to a boil. Gradually stir about 1 cup of hot milk mixture into egg substitute; add to remaining hot milk mixture, stirring constantly. Cook, stirring constantly, 2 additional minutes (do not boil). Remove from heat. Stir in remaining 2 cups milk and vanilla.

Combine cocoa and sugar substitute in a large bowl. Gradually add hot milk mixture, stirring until smooth. Stir in chopped candy. Chill approximately 30 minutes just until cold, stirring occasionally (do not overchill).

Pour chocolate mixture into freezer container of a 4-quart hand-turned or electric freezer and freeze according to manufacturer's instructions. Pack freezer with additional ice and rock salt, and let stand 1 hour before serving.

Per Serving:

Calories 168	Fiber 0.1g
Fat 4.0g (sat 2.3g)	Cholesterol 3mg
Protein 7.6g	Sodium 168mg
Carbohydrate 21.4g	Exchanges: 1 Starch, ½ Skim Milk, 1 Fat

Fudgy Peanut Butter Ice Cream

Yield: 8 (½-cup) servings

1   (1.4-ounce) package chocolate sugar-free, fat-free instant pudding
mix
1   (12-ounce) can evaporated fat-free milk
1½ cups fat-free milk
16 sugar-free chocolate peanut butter cups, chopped (such as Estee
Fructose-Sweetened Peanut Butter Cups)

Combine first 3 ingredients in a large bowl, stirring with a wire whisk until smooth. Stir in chopped candy.

Pour chocolate mixture into freezer container of a 2-quart hand-turned or electric freezer. Freeze according to manufacturer's instructions. Pack freezer with additional ice and rock salt, and let stand at least 1 hour before serving.

Per Serving:

Calories 151	**Fiber** 0.5g
Fat 5.1g (sat 3.1g)	**Cholesterol** 1mg
Protein 7.1g	**Sodium** 279mg
Carbohydrate 20.2g	**Exchanges:** 1 Starch, ½ Skim Milk, 1 Fat

Homemade Peach Ice Cream

Yield: 12 (½-cup) servings

2	cups evaporated fat-free milk
1	cup fat-free milk
⅔	cup granulated sugar substitute with aspartame (such as Equal Spoonful)
½	cup fat-free egg substitute
¼	teaspoon almond extract
1	cup chopped fresh or frozen peaches (about 2 medium peaches)

Combine first 5 ingredients in a large bowl; beat at medium speed of an electric mixer until blended. Stir in peaches.

Pour mixture into freezer container of a 2-quart hand-turned or electric freezer, and freeze according to manufacturer's instructions. Pack freezer with additional ice and rock salt, and let stand at least 1 hour before serving.

Per Serving:

Calories 58	Fiber 0.5g
Fat 0.1g (sat 0.1g)	Cholesterol 2mg
Protein 5.1g	Sodium 75mg
Carbohydrate 10.5g	Exchanges: ½ Fruit, ½ Skim Milk

If you don't have almond extract, use ½ teaspoon vanilla extract.

Frozen Pineapple Yogurt with Raspberries

Yield: 4 (½-cup) servings

1	(20-ounce) can pineapple chunks in juice, drained
½	cup vanilla low-fat yogurt sweetened with aspartame
1	tablespoon granulated sugar substitute (such as Sugar Twin)
1	tablespoon lemon juice
1	cup fresh raspberries

Arrange pineapple on a baking sheet, and freeze 2 hours or until frozen.

Place frozen pineapple in container of an electric blender; cover and process until crushed. Add yogurt, sugar substitute, and lemon juice; process until smooth.

To serve, spoon frozen yogurt mixture evenly into 4 dessert dishes, and top evenly with fresh raspberries.

Per Serving:

Calories 105	Fiber 2.3g
Fat 0.6g (sat 0.3g)	Cholesterol 2mg
Protein 1.6g	Sodium 21mg
Carbohydrate 23.9g	Exchanges: ½ Starch, 1 Fruit

After you freeze the pineapple chunks, this refreshing frozen dessert takes only 5 minutes to make.

Ice Cream Sandwich Dessert

Yield: 12 servings

1½	teaspoons instant coffee granules
1	packet sugar substitute with aspartame (such as Equal packets)
2	tablespoons hot water
1	(8-ounce) container fat-free frozen whipped topping, thawed
6	no-sugar-added, reduced-fat ice cream sandwiches
1	(2.75-ounce) package sugar-free chocolate wafer bars, coarsely chopped (such as Sweet 'N Low)

Dissolve coffee and sugar substitute in hot water, stirring well; let cool slightly. Fold coffee mixture into whipped topping. Set aside.

Arrange 6 ice cream sandwiches in bottom of an 11- x 7- x 1½-inch baking dish. Spread whipped topping mixture evenly over ice cream sandwiches. Sprinkle with chopped wafer bars. Cover and freeze 2 hours or until firm.

To serve, cut into squares, and serve immediately.

Per Serving:

Calories 135	Fiber 0.5g
Fat 3.0g (sat 1.8g)	Cholesterol 5mg
Protein 2.5g	Sodium 86mg
Carbohydrate 24.3g	Exchanges: 1 Starch, ½ Carbohydrate, ½ Fat

No one will know that this scrumptious dessert is sugar free. And if they <u>do</u> figure it out, they won't care because it's so good!

Cookies 'n Cream Crunch

Yield: 9 servings

1	(6½-ounce) package sugar-free chocolate sandwich cookies, crushed
⅓	cup chopped pecans
3	tablespoons reduced-calorie margarine, melted
1	quart vanilla no-sugar-added, fat-free ice cream, softened

Combine first 3 ingredients; reserve 1 cup mixture. Press remaining crumb mixture firmly in bottom of a 9-inch square pan. Freeze 10 minutes.

Spread ice cream over crumb mixture in pan. Sprinkle reserved crumb mixture over ice cream; gently press mixture into ice cream. Cover and freeze at least 8 hours.

To serve, let stand at room temperature 5 minutes; cut into 9 squares.

Per Serving:

Calories 232	Fiber 0.7g
Fat 10.1g (sat 1.7g)	Cholesterol 0mg
Protein 6.3g	Sodium 182mg
Carbohydrate 34.2g	Exchanges: 2 Starch, 2 Fat

Chocolate–Peppermint Ice Cream Cake

Yield: 9 servings

1 (8-ounce) package chocolate sugar-free, low-fat cake
        mix (such as Sweet 'N Low)
Cooking spray
20 sugar-free peppermint candies, finely crushed and divided
        (about ½ cup)
2 cups vanilla no-sugar-added, fat-free ice cream, softened

Prepare cake mix according to package directions. Divide batter between 2 (8-inch) square cake pans coated with cooking spray. Bake at 375° for 10 minutes or until a wooden pick inserted in center comes out clean. Remove layers from pans, and place on a wire rack. Let cool completely.

Stir ¼ cup crushed candies into ice cream. Return 1 cake layer to pan. Spread ice cream mixture over cake layer. Top with remaining cake layer; sprinkle cake with remaining ¼ cup crushed candies. Cover and freeze until firm.

To serve, let stand at room temperature 10 minutes; cut into 9 squares.

Per Serving:

Calories 153	**Fiber** 0.6g
Fat 1.8g (sat 0.6g)	**Cholesterol** 0mg
Protein 3.4g	**Sodium** 48mg
Carbohydrate 40.2g	**Exchanges:** 1 Starch, 1½ Carbohydrate

(Photograph on page 43)

Fish & Shellfish

Zesty Baked Salmon, page 69

Pan-Fried Catfish • Easy Parmesan Flounder • Spicy Grilled Grouper • Hobo Fish Dinner • Sesame-Baked Orange Roughy • Italian Red Snapper • Zesty Baked Salmon Soy-Lime Grilled Tuna • Seasoned Crab Cakes • Steamed Clams • Scallop and Pasta Toss • Barbecued Shrimp Light Shrimp Curry • Lemon-Garlic Shrimp

Pan-Fried Catfish

Yield: 4 servings

½ cup yellow cornmeal
1 teaspoon paprika
½ teaspoon pepper
¼ teaspoon salt
¼ teaspoon onion powder
¼ teaspoon ground celery seeds
¼ teaspoon dry mustard
4 (4-ounce) farm-raised catfish fillets
¼ cup fat-free milk
1 tablespoon vegetable oil

Combine first 7 ingredients. Dip fish in milk; dredge in cornmeal mixture.

Heat oil in a nonstick skillet over medium-high heat. Add fish; cook 3 minutes on each side or until fish flakes easily when tested with a fork.

Serve immediately.

Per Serving:

Calories 234

Fat 8.7g (sat 1.8g)

Protein 22.8g

Carbohydrate 14.8g

Fiber 1.1g

Cholesterol 66mg

Sodium 227mg

Exchanges: 1 Starch, 3 Lean Meat

Easy Parmesan Flounder

Yield: 4 servings

4	(4-ounce) flounder fillets
Cooking spray	
1	tablespoon lemon juice
¼	cup nonfat mayonnaise
3	tablespoons grated Parmesan cheese
1	tablespoon thinly sliced green onions
1	tablespoon reduced-calorie margarine, softened
⅛	teaspoon hot sauce

Place fish on rack of a broiler pan coated with cooking spray; brush with lemon juice. Broil 5½ inches from heat 5 to 6 minutes or until fish flakes easily when tested with a fork.

Combine mayonnaise and remaining 4 ingredients, stirring well. Spread mayonnaise mixture evenly over fish. Broil 1 minute or until lightly browned.

Serve immediately.

Per Serving:

Calories 146	Fiber 0.0g
Fat 4.4g (sat 1.3g)	Cholesterol 61mg
Protein 22.1g	Sodium 378mg
Carbohydrate 3.5g	Exchanges: 3 Very Lean Meat, 1 Fat

Spicy Grilled Grouper

Yield: 6 servings

1½ pounds grouper fillets
¼ cup lemon juice
1½ teaspoons chili powder
¼ teaspoon ground cumin
¼ teaspoon paprika
1 clove garlic, minced
Dash of ground red pepper
Cooking spray

Cut fillets into 6 equal pieces. Place fish in a shallow baking dish. Combine lemon juice and next 5 ingredients, stirring well; pour over fish. Cover and marinate in refrigerator 30 minutes.

Remove fish from marinade, reserving marinade. Place marinade in a small saucepan; bring to a boil, and set aside.

Coat grill rack with cooking spray; place on grill over medium-hot coals (350° to 400°). Coat a wire grilling basket with cooking spray. Place fish in basket, and grill 10 minutes on each side or until fish flakes easily when tested with a fork, basting often with reserved marinade.

Serve immediately.

Per Serving:

Calories 124	Fiber 0.3g
Fat 1.5g (sat 0.3g)	Cholesterol 47mg
Protein 24.8g	Sodium 59mg
Carbohydrate 1.5g	Exchanges: 3 Very Lean Meat

Hobo Fish Dinner

Yield: 4 servings

Cooking spray
1   teaspoon salt-free lemon-herb seasoning (such as Mrs. Dash)
½   teaspoon salt
½   teaspoon dried dillweed
4   small baking potatoes, thinly sliced
3   cups thinly sliced onion (about 2 medium)
1   cup thinly sliced carrot (about 2 medium)
4   (4-ounce) halibut fillets (or any firm white fish)

Coat one side of 4 (18-inch) squares of heavy-duty aluminum foil with cooking spray.

Combine seasoning, salt, and dillweed. Layer potato, onion, and carrot slices evenly in centers of coated foil squares. Sprinkle evenly with seasoning mixture. Place fish over vegetables (Step 1). Fold foil over fish and vegetables; crimp edges to seal (Step 2). Place packets on a baking sheet. Bake at 450° for 30 minutes. Serve immediately.

Per Serving:

Calories 268	Fiber 5.1g
Fat 3.2g (sat 0.4g)	Cholesterol 53mg
Protein 27.8g	Sodium 378mg
Carbohydrate 32.0g	Exchanges: 2 Starch, 3 Very Lean Meat

Wrapping Fish in Foil

Step 1

Step 2

Sesame-Baked Orange Roughy

Yield: 6 servings

6	(4-ounce) orange roughy fillets
2	tablespoons water
1	teaspoon minced gingerroot
1	clove garlic, minced
½	teaspoon lemon juice
½	teaspoon low-sodium soy sauce
¼	teaspoon dried crushed red pepper
2	tablespoons sesame seeds, toasted
Cooking spray	
¼	teaspoon paprika
Lemon slices (optional)	

Place fish in a heavy duty, zip-top plastic bag. Combine water and next 5 ingredients. Pour over fish. Seal bag, and turn to coat fish. Marinate in refrigerator 1 to 2 hours, turning once.

Remove fish from marinade; discard marinade. Sprinkle both sides of each fillet with sesame seeds. Place fish on rack of a broiler pan coated with cooking spray. Broil 3½ inches from heat 6 to 8 minutes or until fish flakes easily when tested with a fork.

Sprinkle fish evenly with paprika. If desired, garnish with lemon slices, and serve with a tossed salad.

Serve immediately.

Per Serving:

Calories 92	Fiber 0.2g
Fat 2.1g (sat 0.2g)	Cholesterol 22mg
Protein 16.6g	Sodium 81mg
Carbohydrate 1.0g	Exchanges: 2 Very Lean Meat

Italian Red Snapper

Yield: 4 servings

4	(4-ounce) red snapper fillets
¼	cup dry white wine or low-sodium chicken broth
¼	cup lemon juice
½	teaspoon dried oregano
½	teaspoon dried basil
¼	teaspoon salt
¼	teaspoon pepper
4	cloves garlic, minced
1	(14½-ounce) can no-salt-added diced tomatoes, drained

Place fish in an 11- x 7- x 1½-inch baking dish. Combine wine (or broth) and next 6 ingredients, stirring well. Pour wine mixture and tomato over fish.

Bake, uncovered, at 350° for 25 minutes or until fish flakes easily when tested with a fork.

Serve immediately.

Per Serving:

Calories 136	Fiber 0.6g
Fat 1.6g (sat 0.3g)	Cholesterol 42mg
Protein 24.1g	Sodium 229mg
Carbohydrate 5.7g	Exchanges: 1 Vegetable, 3 Very Lean Meat

Zesty Baked Salmon

Yield: 4 servings

4 (4-ounce) salmon fillets
Cooking spray
2 tablespoons chopped green onions
1 tablespoon low-fat mayonnaise
1 tablespoon plain nonfat yogurt
1 teaspoon lemon-pepper seasoning
¼ teaspoon salt
¼ teaspoon dry mustard
Chopped green onions (optional)
Lemon slices (optional)

Place fish, skin side down, in a baking dish coated with cooking spray. Bake at 425° for 18 minutes or until fish flakes easily when tested with a fork.

Combine 2 tablespoons green onions and next 5 ingredients; spread evenly over fish. Bake 2 additional minutes or until sauce is bubbly.

Serve immediately. If desired, sprinkle with additional chopped green onions, and garnish with lemon slices.

Per Serving:

Calories 164	**Fiber** 0.0g
Fat 6.0g (sat 2.0g)	**Cholesterol** 70mg
Protein 23.0g	**Sodium** 334mg
Carbohydrate 2.0g	**Exchanges:** 3 Lean Meat

(Photograph on page 61)

Soy-Lime Grilled Tuna

Yield: 4 servings

4	(4-ounce) tuna steaks (1 inch thick)
½	cup lime juice
¼	cup low-sodium soy sauce
1	teaspoon minced gingerroot
½	teaspoon dried crushed red pepper

Cooking spray

Place fish in a heavy-duty, zip-top plastic bag. Combine lime juice and next 3 ingredients, stirring well. Pour lime juice mixture over fish. Seal bag, turning to coat fish. Marinate in refrigerator 30 minutes, turning once.

Remove fish from marinade; reserve marinade. Place marinade in a small saucepan; bring to a boil, and set aside.

Coat grill rack with cooking spray; place on grill over medium-hot coals (350° to 400°). Place fish on rack; grill, covered, 4 to 5 minutes on each side or until fish flakes easily when tested with a fork, basting often with reserved marinade.

Remove from grill, and serve immediately.

Per Serving:

Calories 162	Fiber 0.0g
Fat 5.5g (sat 1.4g)	Cholesterol 42mg
Protein 25.5g	Sodium 140mg
Carbohydrate 0.7g	Exchanges: 3½ Very Lean Meat

Fresh tuna has a distinctly rich-flavored flesh that's so firm it feels almost like meat in the mouth.

SHARON TYLER HERBST, <u>Never Eat More Than You Can Lift</u>

Seasoned Crab Cakes

Yield: 5 servings

1½	cups soft breadcrumbs
2	tablespoons chopped green onions
2	tablespoons chopped sweet red pepper
2	tablespoons nonfat mayonnaise
1	tablespoon finely chopped fresh parsley
½	teaspoon dry mustard
¼	teaspoon ground red pepper
1	egg white
1	pound fresh crabmeat, drained and flaked
	Butter-flavored cooking spray
1	teaspoon vegetable oil
	Lemon wedges (optional)

Combine first 8 ingredients; stir well. Add crabmeat, stirring gently. Shape mixture into 5 patties.

Coat a large nonstick skillet with cooking spray; add oil. Place over medium heat until hot. Add patties; cook 5 minutes on each side or until lightly browned.

Serve immediately. Garnish with lemon wedges, if desired.

Per Serving:

Calories 184	Fiber 0.8g
Fat 3.6g (sat 0.6g)	Cholesterol 86mg
Protein 20.5g	Sodium 469mg
Carbohydrate 16.2g	Exchanges: 1 Starch, 2½ Very Lean Meat

Ready in 20 Minutes!

Steamed Clams

Yield: 4 servings

3	dozen fresh cherrystone clams
¾	cup water
⅓	cup dry white wine or low-sodium chicken broth
1½	tablespoons Old Bay seasoning
½	teaspoon ground white pepper

Lemon wedges (optional)

Scrub clams thoroughly, discarding any that are cracked or open.

Combine water and next 3 ingredients in a large Dutch oven; bring to a boil. Add clams; cover, reduce heat, and simmer 10 to 12 minutes or until clams open. Remove and discard any unopened clams. Remove remaining clams with a slotted spoon, reserving liquid, if desired.

Serve clams immediately. If desired, serve with reserved liquid and lemon wedges.

Per Serving:

Calories 88	Fiber 0.2g
Fat 1.2g (sat 0.1g)	Cholesterol 39mg
Protein 14.6g	Sodium 846mg
Carbohydrate 3.6g	Exchanges: 2 Very Lean Meat

Scallop and Pasta Toss

Yield: 4 servings

Cooking spray
1   tablespoon reduced-calorie margarine
2   cups diagonally sliced celery
1   cup sliced fresh mushrooms
½   cup sliced green onions (about 2 onions)
½   cup sliced carrot
2   cloves garlic, minced
¾   pound fresh bay scallops
2   tablespoons water
2   teaspoons white wine Worcestershire sauce
½   teaspoon ground ginger
¼   teaspoon salt
⅛   teaspoon pepper
4   cups cooked spinach linguine (cooked without salt or fat)

Coat a large nonstick skillet with cooking spray; add margarine. Place over medium-high heat until margarine melts. Add celery and next 4 ingredients; sauté until crisp-tender. Add scallops and next 5 ingredients; cook 5 to 7 minutes or until scallops are opaque, stirring occasionally.

Place linguine in a large serving bowl; add scallop mixture, and toss gently.

Serve immediately.

Per Serving:

Calories 323	Fiber 4.9g
Fat 5.0g (sat 0.7g)	Cholesterol 28mg
Protein 23.3g	Sodium 444mg
Carbohydrate 46.8g	Exchanges: 3 Starch, 2 Very Lean Meat

Barbecued Shrimp

Yield: 4 servings

24   unpeeled jumbo fresh shrimp
Cooking spray
¼   cup chopped onion
½   cup reduced-calorie ketchup
1   tablespoon dried rosemary
1   tablespoon dry mustard
1   tablespoon granulated brown sugar substitute (such as brown
       Sugar Twin)
1   tablespoon white vinegar
¼   teaspoon garlic powder
Dash of hot sauce
4   lemon wedges

Peel and devein shrimp, leaving tails intact. Place shrimp in a large heavy-duty, zip-top plastic bag. Set aside.

Coat a nonstick skillet with cooking spray; place over medium-high heat until hot. Add onion; sauté until tender. Stir in ketchup and next 6 ingredients; pour over shrimp. Seal bag; shake until shrimp is coated. Marinate in refrigerator 1 hour, turning once.

Thread shrimp evenly onto 8-inch skewers, running skewers through necks and tails. Coat grill rack with cooking spray; place on grill over medium-hot coals (350° to 400°). Place skewers on rack; grill, covered, 3 to 4 minutes on each side or until shrimp turn pink.

Squeeze 1 lemon wedge over each skewer, and serve immediately.

Per Serving:

Calories 145	Fiber 0.3g
Fat 2.0g (sat 0.3g)	Cholesterol 221mg
Protein 24.3g	Sodium 266mg
Carbohydrate 5.3g	Exchanges: 3 Very Lean Meat

Light Shrimp Curry

Yield: 6 servings

3 pounds unpeeled medium-size fresh shrimp
Cooking spray
1 tablespoon margarine
1 cup chopped onion
¼ cup minced jalapeño pepper (about 1 pepper)
2 tablespoons minced gingerroot
1 teaspoon minced garlic
2 tablespoons curry powder
2 (14½-ounce) cans no-salt-added stewed tomatoes, undrained
1 (8-ounce) carton plain nonfat yogurt
¼ teaspoon salt
¼ teaspoon ground white pepper
3 cups cooked long-grain rice (cooked without salt or fat)
⅓ cup chopped green onions (about 1½ onions)

Peel and devein shrimp; set aside.

Coat a large nonstick skillet with cooking spray; add margarine. Place over medium-high heat until margarine melts. Add chopped onion, and sauté until tender. Stir in jalapeño pepper, gingerroot, and garlic; sauté 2 minutes. Add curry powder; sauté 2 minutes. Add tomatoes; cook over medium heat 5 minutes or until slightly thickened, stirring often. Stir in yogurt, salt, and pepper. Add shrimp; bring to a boil. Reduce heat, and simmer 5 minutes or until shrimp turn pink.

Spoon mixture over rice; sprinkle with green onions. Serve immediately.

Per Serving:

Calories 331	Fiber 2.0g
Fat 4.5g (sat 0.8g)	Cholesterol 173mg
Protein 29.6g	Sodium 344mg
Carbohydrate 42.4g	Exchanges: 2 Starch, 2 Vegetable, 3 Very Lean Meat

Lemon-Garlic Shrimp

Yield: 6 servings

2¼ pounds unpeeled large fresh shrimp
Cooking spray
3 tablespoons minced onion
3 tablespoons minced fresh parsley
1½ teaspoons minced garlic
½ cup lemon juice
¼ cup fat-free Italian dressing
¼ cup water
¼ cup low-sodium soy sauce
½ teaspoon freshly ground pepper

Peel and devein shrimp, leaving tails intact. Place shrimp in a large, heavy-duty, zip-top plastic bag. Set aside.

Coat a nonstick skillet with cooking spray; place over medium-high heat until hot. Add onion, parsley, and garlic; sauté until tender. Stir in lemon juice and remaining 4 ingredients. Pour mixture over shrimp; seal bag, turning to coat shrimp. Marinate in refrigerator 1 to 2 hours, turning occasionally.

Remove shrimp from marinade, reserving marinade. Broil 5½ inches from heat 5 minutes or until shrimp turn pink, basting with marinade. Serve immediately with a slotted spoon.

Per Serving:

Calories 88	Fiber 0.2g
Fat 1.0g (sat 0.2g)	Cholesterol 157mg
Protein 17.1g	Sodium 289mg
Carbohydrate 1.7g	Exchanges: 2 Very Lean Meat

Meatless Main Dishes

Three-Pepper Pizza, page 89

Potato-Cheddar Omelets • Spinach-Mushroom Omelet
Vegetable Frittata • Vegetable-Cheese Pie • Spinach Lasagna
Black Bean Lasagna Rolls • Vegetable Burritos
Three-Pepper Pizza • Seasoned Vegetable Tacos
Italian Stuffed Eggplant • Roasted Vegetable Pot Pie

Potato-Cheddar Omelets

Yield: 4 servings

Cooking spray
1   cup unpeeled, shredded round red potato (about ½ pound potatoes)
½   cup chopped zucchini
½   cup chopped sweet red pepper
¼   cup sliced green onions (about 1 onion)
1½   cups fat-free egg substitute
¼   cup fat-free milk
½   teaspoon minced fresh oregano
¼   teaspoon pepper
⅛   teaspoon salt
½   cup (2 ounces) shredded reduced-fat Cheddar cheese

Coat a 10-inch nonstick skillet with cooking spray; place over medium-high heat until hot. Add potato and next 3 ingredients; sauté 7 minutes or until tender. Remove from skillet; set aside. Wipe skillet with a paper towel. Combine egg substitute and next 4 ingredients, stirring well.

Coat skillet with cooking spray; place over medium-high heat until hot. Pour half of egg mixture into skillet. As mixture begins to cook, lift edges with a spatula, and tilt pan to allow uncooked portion to flow underneath. When set, spoon half of vegetables over half of omelet. Sprinkle vegetables with half of cheese. Loosen with spatula; fold in half. Cook 1 to 2 minutes or until cheese begins to melt. Slide onto a plate, cut in half, and keep warm. Repeat with remaining ingredients. Serve immediately.

Per Serving:

Calories 136	Fiber 1.4g
Fat 3.1g (sat 1.6g)	Cholesterol 9mg
Protein 15.2g	Sodium 326mg
Carbohydrate 11.8g	Exchanges: 2 Vegetable, 2 Very Lean Meat

Spinach-Mushroom Omelet

Yield: 2 servings

Butter-flavored cooking spray
1   cup sliced fresh mushrooms
1   tablespoon chopped green onions
3   cups loosely packed fresh spinach, coarsely chopped
2   tablespoons tub-style light cream cheese, softened
½   cup fat-free egg substitute
1   egg
⅛   teaspoon salt
⅛   teaspoon pepper
2   tablespoons (½ ounce) shredded reduced-fat Cheddar cheese

Coat a 10-inch nonstick skillet with cooking spray; place over medium-high heat until hot. Add mushrooms and onions; sauté until tender. Remove from skillet; set aside.

Add spinach to skillet; sauté until spinach wilts. Remove from heat; stir in cream cheese. Remove from skillet, and keep warm. Wipe skillet with a paper towel. Combine egg substitute and next 3 ingredients, stirring well.

Coat skillet with cooking spray; place over medium heat until hot. Pour egg mixture into skillet. As mixture begins to cook, lift edges with a spatula, and tilt pan to allow uncooked portion to flow underneath. When set, spoon mushroom mixture, spinach mixture, and Cheddar cheese over half of omelet. Loosen with spatula, and fold in half. Cook 1 to 2 minutes or until cheese begins to melt. Slide onto a plate; cut in half. Serve immediately.

Per Serving:

Calories 145	Fiber 2.5g
Fat 7.0g (sat 3.1g)	Cholesterol 123mg
Protein 15.0g	Sodium 440mg
Carbohydrate 6.2g	Exchanges: 1 Vegetable, 2 Lean Meat

Vegetable Frittata

Yield: 2 servings

1	cup fat-free egg substitute
1	tablespoon fat-free milk
¼	teaspoon dried oregano
⅛	teaspoon garlic powder
⅛	teaspoon salt
⅛	teaspoon pepper

Cooking spray

¼	cup chopped sweet red pepper
¼	cup chopped broccoli flowerets
2	fresh mushrooms, sliced
¼	cup alfalfa sprouts
½	cup (2 ounces) shredded reduced-fat Swiss cheese

Combine first 6 ingredients; set aside.

Coat a small nonstick skillet with cooking spray, and place over medium-high heat until hot. Add red pepper, broccoli, and mushrooms; sauté until tender.

Add egg mixture to skillet; cover and cook over medium-low heat 8 to 10 minutes or until set. Remove from heat; top frittata with alfalfa sprouts, and sprinkle with cheese. Cover and let stand 3 to 5 minutes or until cheese melts. Cut into wedges, and serve immediately.

Per Serving:

Calories 162	Fiber 0.8g
Fat 5.5g (sat 2.8g)	Cholesterol 18mg
Protein 22.6g	Sodium 372mg
Carbohydrate 5.0g	Exchanges: 1 Vegetable, 3 Very Lean Meat

Eggs are very much like small boys. If you overheat them or overbeat them, they will turn on you, and no amount of future love will right the wrong.

IRENA CHALMERS, author

Vegetable-Cheese Pie

Yield: 4 servings

4½   cups frozen shredded hash brown potatoes, thawed
1   cup (4 ounces) shredded reduced-fat Cheddar cheese
¼   cup finely chopped green pepper
¼   cup chopped tomato
3   tablespoons finely chopped onion
¾   cup fat-free milk
¾   cup fat-free egg substitute
½   teaspoon salt
¼   teaspoon pepper
Cooking spray

Combine first 9 ingredients in a large bowl, stirring well. Pour mixture into a 9-inch pie plate coated with cooking spray.

Bake, uncovered, at 350° for 45 minutes or until a knife inserted in center comes out clean.

Let stand 10 minutes before serving.

Per Serving:

Calories 201	Fiber 0.9g
Fat 5.7g (sat 3.2g)	Cholesterol 19mg
Protein 15.9g	Sodium 603mg
Carbohydrate 21.3g	Exchanges: 1 Starch, 1 Vegetable, 2 Lean Meat

Keep a bag of shredded potatoes and a carton of egg substitute in the freezer so you can whip up this pie for a casual brunch or lunch. Vary the vegetables depending on what you have on hand.

Spinach Lasagna

Yield: 8 servings

9	lasagna noodles, uncooked
2	cups 1% low-fat cottage cheese
½	cup fat-free egg substitute
2	(10-ounce) packages frozen chopped spinach, thawed and drained well
1	(25¾-ounce) jar fat-free spaghetti sauce with mushrooms
2	cups (8 ounces) shredded part-skim mozzarella cheese
¼	cup plus 2 tablespoons grated Parmesan cheese

Cook lasagna noodles according to package directions, omitting salt and fat. Combine cottage cheese, egg substitute, and spinach in a medium bowl; stir well.

Spread ½ cup spaghetti sauce in a 13- x 9- x 2-inch baking dish. Place 3 noodles over sauce; spoon one-third of spinach mixture over noodles. Top with one-third of remaining spaghetti sauce, ½ cup mozzarella cheese, and 2 tablespoons Parmesan cheese. Repeat procedure twice. Top with remaining ½ cup mozzarella cheese.

Bake, uncovered, at 350° for 30 to 35 minutes or until thoroughly heated.

Let stand 10 minutes before serving.

Per Serving:

Calories 278	Fiber 3.6g
Fat 6.9g (sat 4.1g)	Cholesterol 22mg
Protein 23.6g	Sodium 803mg
Carbohydrate 30.2g	Exchanges: 2 Starch, 2½ Lean Meat

Black Bean Lasagna Rolls

Yield: 8 servings

8	lasagna noodles, uncooked
1	cup (4 ounces) shredded reduced-fat Monterey Jack cheese
1	(15-ounce) carton part-skim ricotta cheese
1	(4½-ounce) can chopped green chiles, drained
½	teaspoon chili powder
⅛	teaspoon salt
2	cups drained canned no-salt-added black beans
Cooking spray	
1	(15½-ounce) jar no-salt-added salsa
Fresh cilantro sprigs (optional)	

Cook lasagna noodles according to package directions, omitting salt and fat; drain well.

Combine cheeses and next 3 ingredients, stirring well. Spread cheese mixture over one side of each noodle. Spoon black beans evenly over cheese mixture. Roll up noodles, jellyroll fashion, beginning at narrow ends.

Place lasagna rolls, seam sides down, in an 11- x 7- x 1½-inch baking dish coated with cooking spray. Cover and bake at 350° for 25 minutes or until thoroughly heated.

To serve, spoon salsa evenly over rolls, and garnish with cilantro sprigs, if desired.

Per Serving:

Calories 295	Fiber 2.8g
Fat 7.8g (sat 4.3g)	Cholesterol 26mg
Protein 18.8g	Sodium 387mg
Carbohydrate 37.8g	Exchanges: 2 Starch, 1 Vegetable, 2 Lean Meat

Vegetable Burritos

Yield: 4 servings

Cooking spray
1   teaspoon olive oil
2   cups sliced fresh mushrooms
½   cup chopped onion
½   cup chopped green pepper
1   clove garlic, pressed
¾   cup drained canned no-salt-added kidney beans
1   tablespoon chopped ripe olives
⅛   teaspoon black pepper
4   (8-inch) fat-free flour tortillas
¼   cup nonfat sour cream
¾   cup salsa, divided
½   cup (2 ounces) shredded reduced-fat sharp Cheddar cheese

Coat a large nonstick skillet with cooking spray; add oil. Place over medium-high heat until hot. Add mushrooms and next 3 ingredients; sauté until tender. Drain mixture, and transfer to a bowl. Add beans, olives, and black pepper, stirring well.

Spoon one-fourth of bean mixture down center of each tortilla. Top each with 1 tablespoon sour cream, 1 tablespoon salsa, and 2 tablespoons cheese; fold opposite sides over filling.

Wipe skillet with a paper towel. Coat skillet with cooking spray; place over medium-high heat until hot. Place burritos, seam sides down, in skillet; cook 1 minute on each side or until lightly browned. Serve with remaining ½ cup salsa.

Per Serving:

Calories 251	Fiber 4.4g
Fat 4.7g (sat 1.9g)	Cholesterol 9mg
Protein 12.8g	Sodium 607mg
Carbohydrate 30.1g	Exchanges: 2 Starch, 1 Medium-Fat Meat

Three-Pepper Pizza

Yield: 6 servings

¼ teaspoon Italian seasoning
⅓ cup tomato paste
¼ cup water
1 (12-inch) prebaked refrigerated pizza crust
1 cup (4 ounces) shredded part-skim mozzarella cheese
1½ cups diced green, sweet red, and yellow pepper (3 small)
½ medium onion, chopped

Combine seasoning, tomato paste, and water in a small bowl; stir well. Spread on pizza crust. Top evenly with cheese. Sprinkle pepper and onion evenly over cheese.

Bake at 450° for 10 to 12 minutes or until cheese melts.

Cut into wedges, and serve.

Per Serving:

Calories 236	Fiber 2.1g
Fat 6.1g (sat 2.0g)	Cholesterol 10mg
Protein 10.3g	Sodium 352mg
Carbohydrate 36.2g	Exchanges: 2 Starch, 1 Vegetable, ½ High-Fat Meat

(Photograph on page 79)

Slicing and Dicing Peppers

Seasoned Vegetable Tacos

Yield: 8 servings

1½   cups frozen whole-kernel corn, thawed
1   cup chopped zucchini (about 1 medium)
1   cup shredded carrot
1   (15-ounce) can no-salt-added kidney beans, drained and rinsed
2   teaspoons chili powder
½   teaspoon garlic powder
½   teaspoon onion powder
¼   teaspoon salt
¼   teaspoon ground oregano
¼   teaspoon granulated sugar substitute (such as Sugar Twin)
½   cup water
4   cups shredded iceberg lettuce
8   corn taco shells
1   cup chopped tomato (about 1 medium)
1   cup (4 ounces) shredded reduced-fat Cheddar cheese
½   cup nonfat sour cream
½   cup salsa

Combine first 11 ingredients in a large nonstick skillet; bring to a boil. Cook, uncovered, 5 minutes or until vegetables are tender.

Place ½ cup lettuce in each taco shell. Spoon ½ cup corn mixture into each. Top each with 2 tablespoons tomato, 2 tablespoons cheese, 1 tablespoon sour cream, and 1 tablespoon salsa.

Serve immediately.

Per Serving:

Calories 226	Fiber 5.3g
Fat 6.2g (sat 2.1g)	Cholesterol 9mg
Protein 12.8g	Sodium 303mg
Carbohydrate 32.1g	Exchanges: 2 Starch, 1 Medium-Fat Meat

Over-the-hill eggplant betrays its age precisely in the same manner as over-the-hill debutantes: slack skin and slightly puckered posteriors.

DIANE LUCAS, English cookbook author

Italian Stuffed Eggplant

Yield: 4 servings

2   medium eggplants
Garlic-flavored cooking spray
1¼ cups chopped onion
1¼ cups chopped zucchini
1   cup sliced fresh mushrooms
¾   cup chopped green pepper
¾   cup chopped tomato
1   (8-ounce) can no-salt-added tomato sauce
1   cup cooked brown rice (cooked without salt or fat)
¼   cup freshly grated Parmesan cheese
1   tablespoon unsalted sunflower kernels, toasted
1   teaspoon dried Italian seasoning
1   cup (4 ounces) shredded part-skim mozzarella cheese

Wash eggplants; cut each in half lengthwise. Remove pulp, leaving ¼-inch-thick shells. Chop pulp; set aside 2 cups. (Reserve remaining pulp for another use.)

Coat a nonstick skillet with cooking spray; place over medium heat until hot. Add onion and next 3 ingredients; sauté until tender. Stir in 2 cups pulp, tomato, and tomato sauce. Cook, uncovered, 15 minutes. Remove from heat; stir in rice and next 3 ingredients.

Arrange shells in a baking dish coated with cooking spray; spoon vegetable mixture evenly into shells. Bake, uncovered, at 350° for 10 minutes. Sprinkle with mozzarella cheese; bake 5 minutes.

Per Serving:

Calories 244	Fiber 4.9g
Fat 8.3g (sat 4.3g)	Cholesterol 21mg
Protein 14.4g	Sodium 270mg
Carbohydrate 30.1g	Exchanges: 1 Starch, 3 Vegetable, 1 Medium-Fat Meat

Roasted Vegetable Pot Pie

Yield: 6 servings

2	(16-ounce) packages frozen stew vegetables, thawed
2	tablespoons fat-free Italian dressing
1	(25¾-ounce) jar fat-free chunky spaghetti sauce with mushrooms and sweet peppers
1	(15-ounce) can no-salt-added red kidney beans, drained and rinsed
1	(10-ounce) can refrigerated pizza crust dough
1	teaspoon fennel seeds

Combine vegetables and Italian dressing, tossing well. Spoon vegetable mixture onto a large baking sheet. Bake at 450° for 20 minutes or until vegetables are lightly browned, stirring once. Remove from oven. Reduce oven temperature to 375°.

Combine roasted vegetable mixture, spaghetti sauce, and kidney beans, in a 13- x 9- x 2-inch baking dish, stirring well.

Unroll dough onto a work surface; sprinkle dough with fennel seeds. Roll dough to a 14- x 10-inch rectangle; place over vegetable mixture. Bake at 375° for 30 minutes or until lightly browned.

Serve immediately.

Per Serving:

Calories 297	Fiber 5.1g
Fat 1.9g (sat 0.4g)	Cholesterol 0mg
Protein 12.0g	Sodium 875mg
Carbohydrate 57.9g	Exchanges: 3 Starch, 2 Vegetable

Meats

Peppercorn Pork Loin Roast, page 114

Mexican Pizza • Individual Meat Loaves • Beef Kabobs • Beef Stroganoff • Beef and Pepper Stir-Fry • Grilled Flank Steak with Corn Salsa • Picante Pot Roast • Beef Tenderloin with Horseradish Sauce • Artichoke Veal Chops • Grilled Lamb Chops Dijon Parslied Leg of Lamb • Skillet-Barbecued Pork Chops • Easy Pork Parmesan • Grilled Tenderloin with Cream Sauce • Peppercorn Pork Loin Roast • Orange-Baked Ham • Sausage-Egg Casserole

Mexican Pizza

Yield: 6 servings

1	(10-ounce) can refrigerated pizza crust dough
Cooking spray	
½	teaspoon garlic-pepper seasoning
¾	pound lean ground round
¼	cup chopped onion
1	jalapeño pepper, seeded and minced
¼	teaspoon salt
¼	teaspoon ground cumin
1	cup no-salt-added tomato sauce
¾	cup seeded, chopped tomato
1	medium-size green pepper, sliced into rings
3	tablespoons sliced ripe olives
1	cup (4 ounces) shredded reduced-fat Monterey Jack cheese

Pat dough into a 13- x 9-inch rectangle on a baking sheet coated with cooking spray. Sprinkle with garlic pepper. Bake at 425° for 8 to 10 minutes or until bottom of dough is crisp.

Coat a large nonstick skillet with cooking spray; place over medium heat until hot. Add meat and next 4 ingredients; cook until meat is browned, stirring until it crumbles. Drain.

Combine tomato sauce and chopped tomato. Spread over crust, leaving a ½-inch border around edges. Top with meat mixture, pepper rings, and olives. Sprinkle with cheese. Bake at 425° for 5 to 7 minutes or until cheese melts. Serve immediately.

Per Serving:

Calories 299	Fiber 2.0g
Fat 9.8g (sat 3.5g)	Cholesterol 47mg
Protein 22.8g	Sodium 644mg
Carbohydrate 29.1g	Exchanges: 2 Starch, 2 Medium-Fat Meat

Individual Meat Loaves

Yield: 2 servings

½   pound lean ground round
¼   cup fat-free egg substitute
2   tablespoons chopped onion
1   tablespoon soft breadcrumbs
1   tablespoon chopped fresh parsley
¼   teaspoon garlic powder
¼   teaspoon low-sodium Worcestershire sauce
Dash of salt
3   tablespoons ketchup, divided
Cooking spray

Combine first 8 ingredients plus 1 tablespoon ketchup in a medium bowl, stirring well. Shape mixture into 2 (5½-inch) loaves. Place loaves on a rack in a roasting pan coated with cooking spray. Spread 1 tablespoon ketchup over each loaf.

Bake at 350° for 1 hour. Remove from oven; let stand 5 minutes before serving.

Per Serving:

Calories 224
Fat 7.5g (sat 2.6g)
Protein 28.5g
Carbohydrate 10.2g

Fiber 0.6g
Cholesterol 71mg
Sodium 545mg
Exchanges: ½ Starch, 4 Lean Meat

Beef is the soul of cooking.

MARIE-ANTOINE CARÊME, French master chef

Beef Kabobs

Yield: 5 servings

1	(1-pound) beef tenderloin
2	teaspoons Worcestershire sauce
1	medium-size green pepper, cut into 20 squares
10	cherry tomatoes
10	small fresh mushrooms
2	small yellow squash, cut into 10 slices
⅛	teaspoon black pepper
Cooking spray	
¼	teaspoon salt

Cut meat into 20 (¾-inch) cubes. Sprinkle Worcestershire sauce over meat. Thread meat, green pepper, tomatoes, mushrooms, and squash alternately onto 5 (12-inch) skewers. Sprinkle evenly with black pepper.

Coat grill rack with cooking spray; place on grill over medium-hot coals (350° to 400°). Place kabobs on rack, and grill, uncovered, 10 minutes or to desired degree of doneness, turning once. Sprinkle evenly with salt.

Serve immediately.

Per Serving:

Calories 172

Fat 7.1g (sat 3.0g)

Protein 21.2g

Carbohydrate 7.4g

Fiber 2.0g

Cholesterol 52mg

Sodium 187mg

Exchanges: 1 Vegetable, 3 Lean Meat

Beef Stroganoff

Yield: 2 servings

6	ounces lean, boneless sirloin steak
	Cooking spray
1½	cups sliced fresh mushrooms
¼	cup sliced onion
½	teaspoon minced garlic
¼	cup canned no-salt-added beef broth
2	tablespoons no-salt-added tomato sauce
½	teaspoon low-sodium Worcestershire sauce
¼	teaspoon salt
⅛	teaspoon pepper
3	tablespoons low-fat sour cream
1½	cups cooked medium egg noodles (cooked without salt or fat)
2	teaspoons chopped fresh parsley

Slice steak diagonally across grain into ¼-inch-thick strips. Coat a nonstick skillet with cooking spray; place over medium-high heat until hot. Add steak; cook 3 minutes or until steak strips are browned on both sides. Add mushrooms, onion, and garlic; sauté 3 minutes.

Add broth and next 4 ingredients to skillet; bring to a boil. Cover, reduce heat, and simmer 15 minutes or until meat is tender. Remove from heat; stir in sour cream.

To serve, spoon over ¾-cup portions of noodles; sprinkle with parsley.

Per Serving:

Calories 350	Fiber 3.7g
Fat 10.5g (sat 3.8g)	Cholesterol 100mg
Protein 26.0g	Sodium 372mg
Carbohydrate 36.6g	Exchanges: 2½ Starch, 3 Lean Meat

Beef and Pepper Stir-Fry

Yield: 4 servings

1	pound lean, boneless sirloin steak
1	teaspoon olive oil
2	cloves garlic, minced
½	teaspoon dried basil
½	teaspoon black pepper
¼	teaspoon salt
3	medium-size green peppers, seeded and cut into ¼-inch-wide strips
1	tablespoon balsamic vinegar
2	cups cooked long-grain rice (cooked without salt or fat)

Trim fat from steak. Slice steak diagonally across grain into ¼-inch-thick strips. Cut strips into 2-inch pieces; set aside.

Add oil to a large nonstick skillet, and place over medium-high heat until hot. Add meat, garlic, and next 3 ingredients; cook 4 minutes, stirring often. Remove from skillet, and set aside.

Add pepper strips to skillet; cook 6 minutes or until tender, stirring often.

Return meat to skillet, and add vinegar. Cook 2 minutes or until thoroughly heated.

To serve, spoon over ½-cup portions of rice.

Per Serving:

Calories 279	Fiber 3.0g
Fat 7.7g (sat 2.4g)	Cholesterol 69mg
Protein 26.8g	Sodium 221mg
Carbohydrate 24.5g	Exchanges: 1 Starch, 1 Vegetable, 3 Lean Meat

Grilled Flank Steak with Corn Salsa

Yield: 4 servings

1	cup frozen corn, thawed
½	cup drained canned black beans
½	cup finely chopped sweet red pepper
1	jalapeño pepper, seeded and finely chopped
1	clove garlic, crushed
2	tablespoons lime juice
2	teaspoons chopped fresh cilantro
2¼	teaspoons black pepper, divided
1	pound flank steak
½	cup dry red wine
¼	cup lemon juice
3	cloves garlic, crushed
2	tablespoons chopped onion
2	tablespoons Worcestershire sauce

Cooking spray

Combine corn, beans, red pepper, jalapeño, 1 garlic clove, lime juice, cilantro, and ¼ teaspoon black pepper. Cover and chill 8 hours.

Sprinkle steak with remaining 2 teaspoons pepper, and place in a heavy-duty, zip-top plastic bag. Combine wine and next 4 ingredients; pour over steak. Seal bag; marinate in refrigerator 8 hours.

Remove steak from bag; discard marinade. Coat grill rack with cooking spray; place on grill over medium-hot coals (350° to 400°). Place steak on rack; grill, covered, 7 minutes on each side or to desired degree of doneness. Remove from grill; cut into thin slices. Serve with corn salsa.

Per Serving:

Calories 297	Fiber 2.4g
Fat 13.0g (sat 5.6g)	Cholesterol 60mg
Protein 25.4g	Sodium 213mg
Carbohydrate 18.3g	Exchanges: 1 Starch, 3 Medium-Fat Meat

Picante Pot Roast

Yield: 16 servings

1   (4-pound) lean bottom round roast
Cooking spray
1   tablespoon chili powder
1¼   teaspoons ground cumin
1   teaspoon granulated sugar substitute (such as Sugar Twin)
½   teaspoon dried whole oregano
¼   teaspoon ground red pepper
2   medium onions, cut into ¼-inch-thick slices
1   (8-ounce) can no-salt-added tomato sauce
2   cups picante sauce
½   cup water

Trim fat from roast. Coat a Dutch oven with cooking spray; place over medium-high heat until hot. Add roast; cook, turning occasionally, until browned on all sides. Combine chili powder and next 4 ingredients; sprinkle over roast. Add remaining ingredients, and bring to a boil. Cover, reduce heat, and simmer 4½ to 5 hours or until roast is tender.

Transfer roast to a serving platter; serve with sauce mixture.

Per Serving:

Calories 166	Fiber 0.7g
Fat 4.1g (sat 1.5g)	Cholesterol 56mg
Protein 22.9g	Sodium 397mg
Carbohydrate 5.0g	Exchanges: 1 Vegetable, 3 Very Lean Meat

Beef Tenderloin with Horseradish Sauce

Yield: 8 servings

1   (8-ounce) carton nonfat sour cream
¼   cup minced fresh parsley
¼   cup prepared horseradish
1   teaspoon white wine Worcestershire sauce
⅛   teaspoon pepper
1   (2-pound) beef tenderloin
Cooking spray
½   teaspoon salt-free lemon-herb seasoning (such as Mrs. Dash)

Combine first 5 ingredients. Cover and chill at least 1 hour.

Trim fat from tenderloin. Place tenderloin on a rack in a roasting pan coated with cooking spray; sprinkle lemon-herb seasoning over tenderloin. Insert a meat thermometer into thickest part of tenderloin, if desired. Bake at 500° for 35 minutes or until thermometer registers 145° (medium-rare) or 160° (medium).

Let stand 10 minutes before slicing. Serve with horseradish sauce.

Per Serving:

Calories 155	Fiber 0.2g
Fat 6.0g (sat 2.3g)	Cholesterol 54mg
Protein 20.2g	Sodium 75mg
Carbohydrate 3.1g	Exchanges: 3 Lean Meat

Artichoke Veal Chops

Yield: 4 servings

4	(6-ounce) lean veal loin chops (¾ inch thick)
1	teaspoon cracked black pepper

Cooking spray

⅓	cup sliced green pepper
¾	cup sliced sweet orange, red, and yellow pepper
⅓	cup canned fat-free, reduced-sodium chicken broth
¼	teaspoon dried whole thyme
2	cloves garlic, minced
1	(14-ounce) can artichoke hearts, drained and quartered
2	tablespoons chopped fresh parsley

Trim fat from veal chops. Rub cracked pepper over chops.

Coat a large ovenproof nonstick skillet with cooking spray, and place over medium-high heat until hot. Add chops, and cook 3 to 4 minutes on each side or until browned. Remove chops from skillet; set aside. Wipe drippings from skillet with a paper towel.

Place green pepper and next 4 ingredients in skillet. Bring to a boil; reduce heat, and simmer 5 minutes. Stir in artichoke hearts. Return chops to skillet, spooning artichoke mixture over veal chops. Cover and bake at 350° for 25 minutes or until veal is tender.

Sprinkle with chopped parsley, and serve immediately.

Per Serving:

Calories 177	Fiber 1.5g
Fat 4.5g (sat 1.3g)	Cholesterol 91mg
Protein 25.3g	Sodium 285mg
Carbohydrate 8.9g	Exchanges: 2 Vegetable, 3 Very Lean Meat

Grilled Lamb Chops Dijon

Yield: 2 servings

2   (5-ounce) lean lamb loin chops (¾ inch thick)
2   tablespoons dry red wine
2   tablespoons water
1   tablespoon chopped garlic (about 1 large clove)
2   teaspoons dried rosemary, crushed
Cooking spray
2   tablespoons plain nonfat yogurt
1   teaspoon Dijon mustard
1   teaspoon capers
½   teaspoon lemon juice
⅛   teaspoon hot sauce

Trim fat from lamb chops; place chops in a small heavy-duty, zip-top plastic bag. Combine wine and next 3 ingredients; pour over chops. Seal bag, and shake until chops are well coated. Marinate in refrigerator 8 hours, turning bag occasionally.

Remove chops from bag, discarding marinade. Coat grill rack with cooking spray, and place on grill over medium-hot coals (350° to 400°). Place chops on rack; grill, covered, 10 minutes on each side or to desired degree of doneness. Transfer to serving plates, and keep warm.

Combine yogurt and remaining 4 ingredients, stirring well. Spoon yogurt mixture over chops.

Serve immediately.

Per Serving:

Calories 168	Fiber 0.2g
Fat 7.2g (sat 2.3g)	Cholesterol 63mg
Protein 20.9g	Sodium 256mg
Carbohydrate 2.4g	Exchanges: 3 Lean Meat

Parslied Leg of Lamb

Yield: 14 servings

1	cup chopped fresh parsley
½	cup chopped green onions (about 2 onions)
2	teaspoons grated orange rind
⅓	cup orange juice
1	tablespoon chopped hazelnuts or pecans
½	teaspoon pepper
1	(3½-pound) lean, boneless leg of lamb

Cooking spray

Combine first 6 ingredients in container of an electric blender or food processor; cover and process until mixture forms a paste.

Trim fat from lamb, and place lamb in a shallow dish. Rub parsley mixture over lamb. Cover and marinate in refrigerator 8 hours.

Place lamb on a rack in a roasting pan coated with cooking spray. Insert a meat thermometer into thickest part of lamb, if desired. Bake, uncovered, at 325° for 1 hour and 45 minutes or until meat thermometer registers 140° (rare) to 160° (medium).

Transfer lamb to a serving platter. Let stand 15 minutes before serving.

Per Serving:

Calories 155	Fiber 0.3g
Fat 6.5g (sat 2.1g)	Cholesterol 67mg
Protein 21.5g	Sodium 53mg
Carbohydrate 1.4g	Exchanges: 3 Lean Meat

Skillet-Barbecued Pork Chops

Yield: 4 servings

4   (4-ounce) boneless center-cut pork loin chops
Cooking spray
¼   cup minced onion
1   tablespoon minced garlic (about 1 large clove)
1   cup water
½   cup no-salt-added tomato paste
3   tablespoons granulated brown sugar substitute (such as
        brown Sugar Twin)
3   tablespoons low-sodium soy sauce
1   tablespoon lemon juice
⅛   teaspoon salt

Trim fat from chops. Coat a small nonstick skillet with cooking spray, and place over medium-high heat until hot. Add pork chops, and cook 2 minutes on each side or until browned. Remove chops from skillet. Wipe drippings from skillet with a paper towel.

Coat skillet with cooking spray; place over medium-high heat until hot. Add onion and garlic; sauté 1 minute. Add water and remaining 5 ingredients to skillet; stir well. Return chops to skillet; bring to a boil. Reduce heat, and simmer, uncovered, 20 minutes or until tender.

To serve, spoon sauce mixture over pork chops.

Per Serving:

Calories 243	Fiber 1.7g
Fat 11.1g (sat 3.7g)	Cholesterol 74mg
Protein 24.5g	Sodium 444mg
Carbohydrate 9.4g	Exchanges: ½ Starch, 3 Lean Meat

Easy Pork Parmesan

Yield: 4 servings

4   (4-ounce) boneless center-cut pork loin chops
⅓   cup fine, dry breadcrumbs
2   tablespoons grated Parmesan cheese
¼   cup fat-free egg substitute
Cooking spray
1½   cups low-fat spaghetti sauce with garlic and herbs
½   cup (2 ounces) shredded reduced-fat mozzarella cheese

Trim fat from pork chops. Place chops between two sheets of heavy-duty plastic wrap, and flatten to ¼-inch thickness, using a meat mallet or rolling pin.

Combine breadcrumbs and Parmesan cheese in a small bowl. Dip chops in egg substitute; dredge in breadcrumb mixture.

Coat a large ovenproof nonstick skillet with cooking spray; place over medium heat until hot. Add chops, and cook 1 to 2 minutes on each side or until browned. Pour spaghetti sauce over chops. Cover and bake at 350° for 25 minutes or until chops are tender. Uncover; sprinkle with mozzarella cheese. Bake 5 additional minutes or until cheese melts.

Serve immediately.

Per Serving:

Calories 322
Fat 11.8g (sat 4.7g)
Protein 34.6g
Carbohydrate 17.1g

Fiber 2.0g
Cholesterol 79mg
Sodium 614mg
Exchanges: 1 Starch, 4 Lean Meat

Grilled Tenderloin with Cream Sauce

Yield: 6 servings

Cooking spray
2 (¾-pound) pork tenderloins
¾ cup 1% low-fat milk
1½ tablespoons all-purpose flour, divided
3 tablespoons Dijon mustard
2 tablespoons dry white wine or low-sodium chicken broth
¼ cup nonfat sour cream
⅛ teaspoon pepper
Fresh rosemary sprigs (optional)
Grilled vegetables (optional)

Coat grill rack with cooking spray; place on grill over medium-hot coals (350° to 400°). Insert a meat thermometer into thickest part of one tenderloin, if desired. Place tenderloins on rack. Grill, covered, 25 to 30 minutes or until meat thermometer registers 160°, turning occasionally.

Combine milk and flour in a saucepan, stirring until smooth. Cook over medium heat, stirring constantly, until thickened. Stir in mustard and wine or broth; remove from heat. Stir in sour cream and pepper.

Cut tenderloins into ¼-inch thick slices, and serve with cream sauce. Garnish with rosemary sprigs and serve with grilled vegetables, if desired.

Per Serving:

Calories 188	Fiber 0.1g
Fat 5.3g (sat 1.7g)	Cholesterol 86mg
Protein 28.1g	Sodium 307mg
Carbohydrate 4.3g	Exchanges: ½ Skim Milk, 3 Lean Meat

Peppercorn Pork Loin Roast

Yield: 10 servings

1	(2½-pound) lean, boneless pork loin roast
3	tablespoons Dijon mustard
1	tablespoon nonfat buttermilk
2	cups soft whole wheat breadcrumbs
2	tablespoons cracked pepper
2	teaspoons whole assorted peppercorns, crushed
2	teaspoons chopped fresh thyme
¼	teaspoon salt

Cooking spray
Fresh thyme sprigs (optional)

Trim fat from roast. Combine mustard and buttermilk. Spread mustard mixture over roast.

Combine breadcrumbs and next 4 ingredients; press breadcrumb mixture evenly onto roast. Place roast on a rack in a roasting pan coated with cooking spray. Insert a meat thermometer into thickest part of roast, if desired. Bake at 325° for 2 hours or until meat thermometer registers 160°.

Let stand 10 minutes before slicing. Garnish with thyme sprigs, if desired.

Per Serving:

Calories 213	**Fiber** 0.8g
Fat 9.3g (sat 3.0g)	**Cholesterol** 68mg
Protein 24.8g	**Sodium** 323mg
Carbohydrate 6.4g	**Exchanges:** ½ Starch, 3 Lean Meat

(Photograph on page 95)

Orange-Baked Ham

Yield: 16 (2-ounce) slices

1	(2-pound) reduced-fat cooked ham
½	cup orange juice concentrate, thawed
¼	cup water
3	tablespoons granulated brown sugar substitute (such as brown Sugar Twin)
2	teaspoons white wine vinegar
1	teaspoon dry mustard
½	teaspoon grated orange rind
¼	teaspoon ground ginger
Cooking spray	
2	tablespoons whole cloves

Score ham in a diamond design; place in a large heavy-duty, zip-top plastic bag. Combine orange juice concentrate and next 6 ingredients; pour mixture over ham. Seal bag, and shake until ham is well coated. Marinate in refrigerator at least 8 hours, turning bag occasionally.

Remove ham from marinade, reserving marinade. Set aside ½ cup marinade; discard remaining marinade. Place ham on a rack in a roasting pan coated with cooking spray; stud with cloves by pushing the long clove ends into the scored intersections in the ham. Insert a meat thermometer into ham, if desired; brush lightly with reserved marinade. Cover; bake at 325° for 1½ hours or until thermometer registers 140°, basting occasionally with marinade.

Serve warm or chilled.

Per Slice:

Calories 99	Fiber 0.1g
Fat 3.2g (sat 1.0g)	Cholesterol 30mg
Protein 12.1g	Sodium 685mg
Carbohydrate 4.8g	Exchanges: 2 Lean Meat

Sausage-Egg Casserole

Yield: 6 servings

4   (1-inch) slices French bread, cubed
Cooking spray
¾   pound reduced-fat turkey and pork ground sausage
1   cup fat-free egg substitute
1½   cups fat-free milk
¾   cup (3 ounces) shredded reduced-fat Cheddar cheese
¼   teaspoon dry mustard
⅛   teaspoon ground red pepper

Place bread cubes in a 2-quart baking dish coated with cooking spray; set aside.

Cook sausage over medium heat until browned, stirring until it crumbles. Drain and pat dry with paper towels. Sprinkle sausage over bread cubes. Combine egg substitute and remaining ingredients; stir well. Pour egg mixture over sausage. Cover and chill 8 hours.

Bake, uncovered, at 350° for 50 minutes or until set. Serve immediately.

Per Serving:

Calories 290	Fiber 0.4g
Fat 15.0g (sat 5.9g)	Cholesterol 57mg
Protein 22.0g	Sodium 723mg
Carbohydrate 14.4g	Exchanges: 1 Starch, 3 Medium-Fat Meat

Roasted Turkey Breast, page 138

Poultry

Chicken Dumpling Pie • Wild Rice and Chicken Casserole
Chicken Curry • Spicy Chicken Strips • Cashew Chicken
Cordon Bleu Casserole • Chicken Fajitas • Ham and Cheese Chicken
Crispy Cheese-Filled Chicken • Grilled Firecracker Chicken
Grilled Lime Chicken • Chicken in Mustard Sauce • Raspberry-
Orange Chicken • Turkey French Bread Pizzas • Turkey Piccata
Rosemary Turkey Tenderloins • Roasted Turkey Breast

Chicken Dumpling Pie

Yield: 8 servings

3   cups chopped, cooked chicken breast
2   cups frozen mixed vegetables, thawed and drained
2   (10¾-ounce) cans reduced-fat, reduced-sodium cream
       of chicken soup
1   (10½-ounce) can low-sodium chicken broth
½   teaspoon poultry seasoning
Cooking spray
2   cups reduced-fat biscuit and baking mix (such as Bisquick)
1   cup fat-free milk
1   (8-ounce) carton low-fat sour cream

Combine first 5 ingredients in a large bowl, stirring well. Pour chicken mixture into a 13- x 9- x 2-inch baking dish coated with cooking spray.

Combine biscuit mix, milk, and sour cream in a medium bowl; spoon over chicken mixture.

Bake, uncovered, at 350° for 50 to 60 minutes or until topping is golden. Serve immediately.

Per Serving:

Calories 328	Fiber 2.2g
Fat 9.2g (sat 3.7g)	Cholesterol 61mg
Protein 22.8g	Sodium 740mg
Carbohydrate 36.0g	Exchanges: 2 Starch, 1 Vegetable, 2 Medium-Fat Meat

Wild Rice and Chicken Casserole

Yield: 6 (1-cup) servings

1   (4-ounce) package boil-in-bag long-grain and wild rice mix
1   (10¾-ounce) can reduced-fat, reduced-sodium cream of
        mushroom soup
¼   cup dry white wine or low-sodium chicken broth
Cooking spray
½   cup sliced fresh mushrooms
½   cup sliced green onions
4   cups chopped, cooked chicken breast
2   tablespoons chopped fresh parsley
¼   teaspoon salt
1   (2-ounce) jar diced pimiento, drained

Cook rice according to package directions, omitting seasoning packet. Combine soup and wine (or broth) in a saucepan; cook over medium heat until heated.

Coat a small skillet with cooking spray; place over medium heat until hot. Add mushrooms and onions; sauté 2 to 3 minutes or until tender.

Combine rice, soup mixture, mushroom mixture, chicken, and remaining ingredients, stirring well. Spoon mixture into a 1½-quart baking dish coated with cooking spray. Bake at 350° for 15 minutes or until thoroughly heated. Serve immediately.

Per Serving:

Calories 260	Fiber 0.3g
Fat 4.6g (sat 1.4g)	Cholesterol 83mg
Protein 31.2g	Sodium 686mg
Carbohydrate 21.2g	Exchanges: 1 Starch, 1 Vegetable, 4 Very Lean Meat

Chicken Curry

Yield: 2 servings

Butter-flavored cooking spray
1   teaspoon reduced-calorie margarine
¼   cup chopped onion
½   cup low-sodium chicken broth
¼   cup fat-free milk
1   tablespoon all-purpose flour
1   teaspoon curry powder
1   cup chopped cooked chicken breast
1   tablespoon lemon juice
¼   teaspoon salt
1   cup cooked long-grain rice (cooked without salt or fat)
¼   cup peeled, chopped banana
1   tablespoon chutney
1   tablespoon chopped unsalted dry-roasted peanuts
2   tablespoons chopped green onions

Coat a medium nonstick skillet with cooking spray; add margarine. Place over medium-high heat until margarine melts. Add ¼ cup onion; sauté until tender.

Combine broth and next 3 ingredients; stir until smooth. Add to onion mixture. Cook over medium heat, stirring constantly, until thickened. Add chicken, lemon juice, and salt. Cook over medium heat 6 minutes or until thoroughly heated, stirring occasionally.

Spoon chicken mixture over rice. Top evenly with banana, chutney, peanuts, and green onions. Serve immediately.

Per Serving:

Calories 381	Fiber 2.5g
Fat 8.0g (sat 1.3g)	Cholesterol 73mg
Protein 32.6g	Sodium 430mg
Carbohydrate 44.3g	Exchanges: 2 Starch, 1 Fruit, 4 Lean Meat

Spicy Chicken Strips

Yield: 4 servings

4	(4-ounce) skinned, boned chicken breast halves
1	(8-ounce) carton plain nonfat yogurt
2	tablespoons lemon juice
½	teaspoon chili powder
½	teaspoon garlic powder
¼	teaspoon ground cumin
1	cup crushed baked tortilla chips

Cooking spray

Cut chicken into 1-inch strips; set aside. Combine yogurt and next 4 ingredients in a medium bowl; stir well. Add chicken strips, and toss to coat. Cover and marinate in refrigerator 8 hours, stirring occasionally.

Remove chicken from marinade, discarding marinade. Dredge chicken strips in tortilla crumbs. Place chicken on a baking sheet coated with cooking spray. Bake at 350° for 35 minutes or until lightly browned and crisp.

Serve immediately.

Per Serving:

Calories 232	Fiber 1.4g
Fat 2.7g (sat 0.5g)	Cholesterol 67mg
Protein 30.8g	Sodium 240mg
Carbohydrate 19.9g	Exchanges: 1 Starch, 4 Very Lean Meat

Cashew Chicken

Yield: 6 servings (serving size: ¾ cup chicken mixture and ½ cup rice)

1	pound skinned, boned chicken breasts, cut into strips
¼	cup orange juice
1	tablespoon plus 1 teaspoon cornstarch, divided
1	teaspoon vegetable oil
¼	cup chopped cashews
1	(8-ounce) can sliced water chestnuts, drained
1	cup chopped green pepper
½	cup chopped green onions
1	tablespoon minced gingerroot
1	cup fat-free, reduced-sodium chicken broth
2	tablespoons low-sodium soy sauce
1	(11-ounce) can mandarin oranges in light syrup, drained
3	cups cooked brown rice (cooked without salt or fat)

Combine chicken strips, orange juice, and 1 teaspoon cornstarch in a medium bowl; cover and chill 1 hour.

Heat oil in a nonstick skillet over medium heat. Add cashews; cook, stirring constantly, 30 seconds. Remove from skillet; set aside. Add chicken mixture to skillet. Cook, uncovered, over medium-high heat 8 minutes or until chicken is lightly browned, stirring constantly. Add water chestnuts and next 3 ingredients; cook 5 minutes.

Combine broth, soy sauce, and 1 tablespoon cornstarch; add to chicken mixture. Bring to a boil; reduce heat, and cook, stirring constantly, until thickened. Remove from heat; stir in oranges. Spoon chicken mixture over rice, and sprinkle with cashews. Serve immediately.

Per Serving:

Calories 311	Fiber 1.3g
Fat 5.3g (sat 0.9g)	Cholesterol 44mg
Protein 22.4g	Sodium 275mg
Carbohydrate 42.8g	Exchanges: 2 Starch, 2 Vegetable, 2 Lean Meat

Cordon Bleu Casserole

Yield: 6 servings

6   (4-ounce) skinned, boned chicken breast halves
Butter-flavored cooking spray
3   (1-ounce) slices reduced-fat, low-salt ham, cut in half
3   (1¼-ounce) slices reduced-fat Swiss cheese, cut in half
2   cups sliced fresh mushrooms
1   (10¾-ounce) can reduced-fat, reduced-sodium cream of
         mushroom soup
3   tablespoons dry sherry or low-sodium chicken broth
1½ cups reduced-sodium chicken-flavored stuffing mix

Arrange chicken in a 13- x 9- x 2-inch baking dish coated with cooking spray. Top chicken with ham and cheese.

Coat a nonstick skillet with cooking spray; place over medium-high heat until hot. Add mushrooms; sauté 5 minutes or until tender. Combine mushrooms, soup, and sherry (or broth). Spoon mixture over chicken. Top with stuffing mix; coat well with cooking spray. Bake at 350° for 45 minutes.

Serve warm.

Per Serving:

Calories 304	Fiber 1.4g
Fat 8.0g (sat 3.8g)	Cholesterol 91mg
Protein 38.0g	Sodium 665mg
Carbohydrate 20.7g	Exchanges: 1½ Starch, 5 Lean Meat

Chicken Fajitas

Yield: 8 servings

2   pounds skinned, boned chicken breasts
¼   cup white wine vinegar
¼   cup lime juice
2   tablespoons low-sodium Worcestershire sauce
2   tablespoons chopped onion
¼   teaspoon ground cumin
2   cloves garlic, minced
Cooking spray
8   (8-inch) flour tortillas
½   cup salsa
½   cup plain low-fat yogurt
¼   cup chopped green chiles

Place chicken between 2 sheets of heavy-duty plastic wrap; flatten to ¼-inch thickness, using a meat mallet or rolling pin. Place chicken in a 13- x 9- x 2-inch baking dish. Combine vinegar and next 5 ingredients; pour over chicken. Cover and refrigerate 4 hours.

Remove chicken from marinade; discard marinade. Coat grill rack with cooking spray; place on grill over medium-hot coals (350° to 400°). Place chicken on rack; grill, covered, 4 minutes on each side or until done. Remove chicken from grill; slice into strips.

Wrap tortillas in aluminum foil; bake at 325° for 15 minutes. Arrange chicken strips evenly in centers of tortillas; top with salsa, yogurt, and chiles. Roll up tortillas, and serve immediately.

Per Serving:

Calories 304	Fiber 1.9g
Fat 6.4g (sat 1.5g)	Cholesterol 73mg
Protein 31.3g	Sodium 347mg
Carbohydrate 28.3g	Exchanges: 2 Starch, 3 Lean Meat

"I hope to make France so prosperous that every peasant will have a chicken in his pot on Sunday."

HENRY IV, King of France, 1589-1610

Ham and Cheese Chicken

Yield: 4 servings

4   (4-ounce) skinned, boned chicken breast halves
¼   teaspoon pepper
1   ounce very thinly sliced lean cooked ham
1   tablespoon plus 1 teaspoon reduced-fat garlic-flavored cream cheese
3   tablespoons fine, dry breadcrumbs
1   teaspoon dried Italian seasoning
1   teaspoon grated Parmesan cheese
½   cup fat-free milk
Cooking spray
1   tablespoon plus 1 teaspoon reduced-calorie margarine, melted
2   teaspoons lemon juice
Dash of paprika

Place chicken between 2 sheets of heavy-duty plastic wrap; flatten to ¼-inch thickness, using a rolling pin. Sprinkle with pepper.

Place one-fourth of ham on each chicken breast half. Spread cream cheese evenly over ham. Roll up chicken, starting with short end and tucking ends under. Secure with wooden picks.

Combine breadcrumbs, Italian seasoning, and Parmesan cheese. Dip chicken rolls in milk, and dredge in breadcrumb mixture. Place, seam side down, in a baking dish coated with cooking spray. Combine margarine and lemon juice; drizzle over chicken. Sprinkle with paprika. Bake, uncovered, at 350° for 30 minutes or until tender. To serve, remove wooden picks, and slice.

Per Serving:

Calories 192	Fiber 0.4g
Fat 5.7g (sat 1.4g)	Cholesterol 72mg
Protein 29.1g	Sodium 283mg
Carbohydrate 4.8g	Exchanges: 4 Very Lean Meat

Crispy Cheese-Filled Chicken

Yield: 4 servings

4   (6-ounce) skinned chicken breast halves
3   ounces reduced-fat extra-sharp Cheddar cheese
1   tablespoon Dijon mustard
1   cup crushed corn flakes crumbs
2   teaspoons salt-free lemon-herb seasoning (such as Mrs. Dash)
½   cup nonfat buttermilk
Cooking spray

Cut a 2-inch-long slit in side of meaty portion of each breast without cutting all the way through the breast (Step 1). Slice cheese into 4 portions; brush with mustard. Place 1 cheese slice in each slit (Step 2); secure with wooden picks.

Combine crumbs and seasoning. Dip chicken in buttermilk; dredge in crumb mixture. Place chicken in a 13- x 9- x 2-inch baking dish coated with cooking spray. Bake at 375° for 1 hour. Remove picks, and serve immediately.

Per Serving:

Calories 317	**Fiber** 0.3g
Fat 6.0g (sat 2.8g)	**Cholesterol** 80mg
Protein 35.8g	**Sodium** 654mg
Carbohydrate 27.7g	**Exchanges:** 2 Starch, 4 Very Lean Meat

Making a Chicken Pocket

Step 1

Step 2

Ready in 30 Minutes!

Grilled Firecracker Chicken

Yield: 4 servings

⅓ cup no-salt-added tomato sauce
¼ cup no-sugar-added apple jelly
2 tablespoons lemon juice
⅛ teaspoon garlic powder
Dash of salt
6 slices canned jalapeño peppers
4 (4-ounce) skinned, boned chicken breast halves
Cooking spray

Combine first 6 ingredients in container of an electric blender or food processor; cover and process until smooth.

Place chicken in a heavy-duty, zip-top plastic bag. Add ¼ cup tomato sauce mixture, reserving remaining tomato sauce mixture. Seal bag, and shake until chicken is well coated. Marinate in refrigerator at least 15 minutes.

Remove chicken from marinade, discarding marinade. Coat grill rack with cooking spray, and place on grill over medium-hot coals (350° to 400°). Place chicken on rack; grill, covered, 5 minutes on each side or until done.

Remove chicken from grill, and serve with reserved tomato sauce mixture.

Per Serving:

Calories 168	Fiber 0.3g
Fat 3.2g (sat 0.9g)	Cholesterol 72mg
Protein 26.6g	Sodium 128mg
Carbohydrate 6.5g	Exchanges: 1 Vegetable, 3½ Very Lean Meat

Grilled Lime Chicken

Yield: 6 servings

1	cup dry white wine or low-sodium chicken broth
¼	cup chopped fresh parsley
½	teaspoon grated lime rind
2	tablespoons fresh lime juice
½	teaspoon freshly ground pepper
6	(4-ounce) skinned, boned chicken breast halves

Cooking spray

Combine first 5 ingredients in a shallow baking dish. Add chicken, turning to coat. Cover and marinate in refrigerator 1 hour.

Remove chicken from marinade, reserving marinade. Place marinade in a small saucepan; bring to a boil, and remove from heat. Coat grill rack with cooking spray; place on grill over medium-hot coals (350° to 400°). Place chicken on rack, and grill, covered, 5 minutes on each side or until done, basting with marinade.

Remove from grill, and serve immediately.

Per Serving:

Calories 142	Fiber 0.2g
Fat 3.0g (sat 0.8g)	Cholesterol 70mg
Protein 25.9g	Sodium 66mg
Carbohydrate 1.3g	Exchanges: 4 Very Lean Meat

Chicken in Mustard Sauce

Yield: 4 servings

½ teaspoon paprika
¼ teaspoon salt
¼ teaspoon coarsely ground pepper
4 (4-ounce) skinned, boned chicken breast halves
Cooking spray
¼ cup dry white wine or low-sodium chicken broth
1½ tablespoons all-purpose flour
¾ cup 1% low-fat milk, divided
1 tablespoon prepared mustard

Combine first 3 ingredients; sprinkle over chicken. Coat a non-stick skillet with cooking spray; place over medium-high heat until hot. Add chicken; cook 3 to 5 minutes on each side or until browned. Remove chicken from skillet, and set aside.

Add wine (or broth) to skillet; deglaze by scraping particles that cling to bottom. Combine flour and ¼ cup milk, stirring until smooth; add to skillet. Stir in remaining ½ cup milk and mustard. Cook over medium heat, stirring constantly, until thickened. Return chicken to skillet. Bring to a boil; cover, reduce heat, and simmer 5 minutes or until chicken is done.

To serve, spoon sauce over chicken, and serve immediately.

Per Serving:

Calories 163	Fiber 0.2g
Fat 2.4g (sat 0.7g)	Cholesterol 68mg
Protein 28.1g	Sodium 356mg
Carbohydrate 5.1g	Exchanges: 4 Very Lean Meat

Poultry is for the cook what canvas is for the painter.

JEAN-ANTHELME BRILLAT-SALVARIN,
French food writer and politician

poultry

Raspberry-Orange Chicken

Yield: 6 servings

1   (3-pound) broiler-fryer, skinned
Butter-flavored cooking spray
1   (10¼-ounce) jar low-sugar orange marmalade
¼   cup raspberry vinegar
½   teaspoon dried whole thyme

Remove giblets and neck from chicken, and reserve for other uses. Rinse chicken under cold, running water, and pat dry. Place chicken, breast side up, on a rack in a roasting pan coated with cooking spray. Truss chicken. Insert a meat thermometer in meaty part of thigh, making sure it does not touch bone. Bake, uncovered, at 375° for 45 minutes.

While chicken bakes, combine marmalade, vinegar, and thyme in a small saucepan. Cook over medium heat until heated and smooth, stirring occasionally. Divide marmalade mixture in half. Set aside half to serve with chicken.

Brush chicken with remaining half of marmalade mixture. Bake 45 additional minutes or until thermometer registers 185°, basting frequently with marmalade mixture.

Reheat reserved marmalade mixture over medium heat until warm, stirring occasionally. To serve, spoon marmalade mixture over chicken.

Per Serving:

Calories 170	Fiber 0.1g
Fat 6.2g (sat 1.7g)	Cholesterol 73mg
Protein 24.0g	Sodium 78mg
Carbohydrate 3.1g	Exchanges: 3 Lean Meat

Turkey French Bread Pizzas

Yield: 8 servings

Cooking spray
1½ pounds freshly ground raw turkey breast
1½ cups sliced fresh mushrooms
¾ cup chopped onion
1 clove garlic, crushed
1 (15-ounce) can pizza sauce
⅛ teaspoon salt
2 (8-ounce) loaves French bread
1½ cups (6 ounces) shredded part-skim mozzarella cheese

Coat a large nonstick skillet with cooking spray; place over medium-high heat until hot. Add turkey and next 3 ingredients. Cook until turkey is browned, stirring until it crumbles. Drain, if necessary. Stir in pizza sauce and salt; cook until thoroughly heated.

Cut each loaf in half horizontally; cut each horizontal piece in half crosswise. Place on an ungreased baking sheet, cut sides up. Broil 5½ inches from heat 1 minute or until lightly toasted. Spoon turkey mixture over French bread pieces; sprinkle with cheese. Broil until cheese melts.

Per Serving:

Calories 355	Fiber 3.0g
Fat 8.4g (sat 3.3g)	Cholesterol 56mg
Protein 30.7g	Sodium 638mg
Carbohydrate 37.6g	Exchanges: 2 Starch, 1 Vegetable, 3 Lean Meat

Turkey Piccata

Yield: 2 servings

2	tablespoons lemon juice, divided
½	pound turkey breast cutlets
1½	tablespoons all-purpose flour
½	teaspoon paprika
¼	teaspoon ground white pepper
½	teaspoon olive oil
¼	cup dry white wine or low-sodium chicken broth
1	tablespoon drained capers
1½	teaspoons chopped fresh parsley

Drizzle 1 tablespoon lemon juice evenly over cutlets; set aside. Combine flour, paprika, and pepper; dredge cutlets in flour mixture.

Heat oil in a medium-size nonstick skillet over medium-high heat. Add turkey; cook 2 minutes on each side or until browned. Transfer turkey to a serving platter; set aside, and keep warm.

Combine wine (or broth) and remaining 1 tablespoon lemon juice in skillet; bring to a boil over medium heat, stirring constantly. Add capers, and cook 1 minute.

To serve, pour caper mixture over cutlets; sprinkle with parsley.

Per Serving:

Calories 189	Fiber 0.3g
Fat 3.0g (sat 0.7g)	Cholesterol 68mg
Protein 27.7g	Sodium 520mg
Carbohydrate 6.6g	Exchanges: ½ Starch, 4 Very Lean Meat

Rosemary Turkey Tenderloins

Yield: 6 servings

3	(½-pound) turkey tenderloins
1½	tablespoons finely chopped fresh rosemary (or 2 teaspoons dried)
1	tablespoon olive oil
1	large clove garlic, minced
¼	teaspoon coarsely ground pepper
¼	teaspoon salt
Cooking spray	
3	tablespoons dry vermouth or low-sodium chicken broth
2	tablespoons water
1	teaspoon cornstarch
Fresh rosemary sprigs (optional)	

Trim fat from turkey. Combine rosemary and next 4 ingredients, stirring well. Rub mixture evenly over both sides of turkey.

Coat a nonstick skillet with cooking spray; place over medium-high heat until hot. Add turkey; cook 7 to 8 minutes on each side or until done. Slice turkey diagonally across grain into thin slices. Arrange slices on a serving platter; keep warm.

Combine vermouth (or broth), water, and cornstarch, stirring well; add to skillet. Bring to a boil; reduce heat, and simmer 1 minute or until thickened, stirring constantly.

To serve, spoon sauce evenly over turkey, and garnish with fresh rosemary, if desired.

Per Serving:

Calories 158	Fiber 0.2g
Fat 4.2g (sat 0.9g)	Cholesterol 68mg
Protein 26.8g	Sodium 170mg
Carbohydrate 1.6g	Exchanges: 4 Very Lean Meat

Roasted Turkey Breast

Yield: 12 servings (serving size: 3 ounces turkey)

1   (5½-pound) turkey breast
Cooking spray
1   teaspoon vegetable oil
Assorted fresh herbs (optional)

Trim fat from turkey. Rinse turkey under cold water, and pat dry.

Place turkey, skin side up, on a rack in a roasting pan coated with cooking spray. Brush turkey lightly with oil. Insert a meat thermometer into meaty part of breast, making sure it does not touch bone. Bake at 325° for 2 to 2¼ hours or until thermometer registers 170°. Let turkey stand 15 minutes before slicing.

To serve, place turkey on a platter, and garnish with fresh herbs, if desired. Remove and discard skin from turkey before eating.

Per Serving:

Calories 146	Fiber 0.0g
Fat 3.3g (sat 0.9g)	Cholesterol 63mg
Protein 26.9g	Sodium 58mg
Carbohydrate 0.0g	Exchanges: 4 Very Lean Meat

(Photograph on page 117)

Salads

Grilled Chicken Caesar Salad, page 157

Fresh Fruit Salad • Melon-Cucumber Salad • Grapefruit and Greens • Orange-Pecan Mixed Green Salad • Cornbread Salad Colorful Coleslaw • Three-Bean Salad • Mexican Corn Salad Confetti Rice Salad • Tabbouleh • Jalapeño Potato Salad Garden Pasta Salad • Fruited Chicken Salad • Grilled Chicken Caesar Salad • Taco Salad Supreme • Grilled Salmon on Greens

Fresh Fruit Salad

Yield: 7 (1-cup) servings

1	(8-ounce) carton low-fat sour cream
2	tablespoons granulated brown sugar substitute (such as brown Sugar Twin)
½	teaspoon ground cinnamon
1¾	cups sliced banana (about 2 small)
1½	cups chopped apple (about 2 small)
1½	cups chopped pear (about 2 medium)
1¼	cups fresh orange sections (about 2 medium)

Combine first 3 ingredients, stirring well. Combine banana and remaining 3 ingredients in a large bowl; toss well.

To serve, spoon 1 cup fruit mixture into each of 7 bowls; top evenly with sour cream mixture.

Per Serving:

Calories 145	Fiber 4.9g
Fat 4.4g (sat 2.5g)	Cholesterol 12mg
Protein 2.0g	Sodium 18mg
Carbohydrate 27.1g	Exchanges: 2 Fruit, 1 Fat

Melon-Cucumber Salad

Yield: 4 (1-cup) servings

1	medium cucumber
3	cups cubed cantaloupe
2	tablespoons frozen pineapple juice concentrate
1	tablespoon water
1	teaspoon vegetable oil
½	teaspoon chili powder

Cut cucumber in half lengthwise; cut each half crosswise into ¼-inch-thick slices. Combine cucumber and cantaloupe in a medium bowl.

Combine pineapple juice concentrate and remaining 3 ingredients, stirring well. Pour mixture over cantaloupe mixture; toss lightly. Cover and chill at least 1 hour.

Toss lightly before serving.

Per Serving:

Calories 77	Fiber 2.1g
Fat 1.6g (sat 0.4g)	Cholesterol 0mg
Protein 1.6g	Sodium 15mg
Carbohydrate 15.8g	Exchange: 1 Fruit

Grapefruit and Greens

Yield: 4 servings

⅓	cup grapefruit juice
2	tablespoons white wine vinegar
½	teaspoon olive oil
¼	teaspoon salt
¼	teaspoon pepper
1	packet sugar substitute with aspartame (such as Equal packets)
4	cups mixed salad greens
2	large pink grapefruit, peeled and sectioned
1	green onion, thinly sliced

Combine first 6 ingredients in a small bowl; set aside.

Place 1 cup salad greens on each of 4 plates. Arrange grapefruit sections evenly on greens, and sprinkle evenly with green onions. Stir juice mixture until well blended; spoon 2 tablespoons dressing over each salad.

Per Serving:

Calories 119	Fiber 1.5g
Fat 1.1g (sat 0.1g)	Cholesterol 0mg
Protein 2.1g	Sodium 152mg
Carbohydrate 25.4g	Exchanges: 1 Fruit, 2 Vegetable

Section the grapefruit over a bowl, then use the juice to make the dressing for this salad.

Orange-Pecan Mixed Green Salad

Yield: 4 servings

¼   cup balsamic vinegar
¼   cup water
1   tablespoon minced onion
1   teaspoon olive oil
¾   teaspoon cornstarch
4   cups mixed salad greens
1   large navel orange, peeled and cut into ¼-inch-thick slices
2   tablespoons chopped pecans

Combine first 5 ingredients in a 2-cup glass measure; stir well. Microwave, uncovered, at HIGH 1 minute or until mixture boils and is slightly thickened. Stir until smooth. Let cool to room temperature.

Place 1 cup salad greens on each of 4 plates. Drizzle evenly with vinegar mixture. Cut orange slices in half. Arrange slices over salad greens, and sprinkle with pecans.

Per Serving:

Calories 61	Fiber 2.6g
Fat 3.8g (sat 0.4g)	Cholesterol 0mg
Protein 1.5g	Sodium 5mg
Carbohydrate 6.5g	Exchanges: 1 Vegetable, 1 Fat

For a richer, nuttier salad, toast the pecans in a skillet over medium heat 5 minutes, stirring often.

Cornbread Salad

Yield: 6 (2-cup) servings

1	(7.5-ounce) package corn muffin mix
6	cups torn romaine lettuce
1	cup seeded, chopped tomato (about 1 medium)
1	cup chopped green pepper (about 1 medium)
¾	cup chopped purple onion (about 1 small)
3	slices turkey bacon, cooked and crumbled
⅔	cup fat-free Ranch-style dressing

Prepare muffin mix according to package directions in an 8-inch square pan, using water instead of milk. Cool in pan 10 minutes. Remove cornbread from pan; cut into cubes.

Place cornbread cubes on a baking sheet; bake at 400° for 10 minutes or until crisp and lightly browned. Place half of cornbread cubes in a large bowl; reserve remaining cornbread cubes for another use.

Combine toasted cornbread cubes, lettuce, and next 4 ingredients; toss well. Pour dressing over salad, and toss well.

Serve immediately.

Per Serving:

Calories 152	Fiber 1.8g
Fat 2.6g (sat 0.5g)	Cholesterol 5mg
Protein 4.1g	Sodium 501mg
Carbohydrate 27.7g	Exchanges: 1 Starch, 2 Vegetable

The cornbread croutons are the best part
of this bacon, lettuce, and tomato salad.

Colorful Coleslaw

Yield: 5 (1-cup) servings

1   (8.5-ounce) package preshredded coleslaw mix (6 cups)
1   cup frozen whole-kernel corn, thawed
¾   cup chopped purple onion
¾   cup chopped sweet red pepper
⅓   cup white vinegar
2   tablespoons granulated sugar substitute (such as Sugar Twin)
1   teaspoon celery seeds
½   teaspoon salt
½   teaspoon chicken-flavored bouillon granules
¼   teaspoon mustard seeds
1   tablespoon water
2   teaspoons vegetable oil
Dash of hot sauce

Remove dressing packet from coleslaw mix; reserve for another use. Combine coleslaw mix and next 3 ingredients in a large bowl; toss well.

Combine vinegar and remaining 8 ingredients in a small saucepan. Bring to a boil, stirring constantly until sugar substitute dissolves. Pour over coleslaw mixture; toss well. Cover and chill at least 2 hours.

Toss before serving. Serve with a slotted spoon.

Per Serving:

Calories 82	Fiber 2.9g
Fat 2.6g (sat 0.4g)	Cholesterol 0mg
Protein 2.2g	Sodium 340mg
Carbohydrate 14.9g	Exchanges: 1 Starch, ½ Fat

Three-Bean Salad

Yield: 10 (½-cup) servings

1	(16-ounce) can no-salt-added green beans, drained
1	(16-ounce) can wax beans, drained
1	(15-ounce) can no-salt-added kidney beans, rinsed and drained
1	medium-size green pepper, chopped
4	green onions, chopped
⅔	cup unsweetened apple juice
⅓	cup cider vinegar
½	teaspoon pepper
¼	teaspoon dry mustard
¼	teaspoon paprika
⅛	teaspoon dried whole oregano

Combine first 5 ingredients in a large bowl, stirring gently.

Combine apple juice and remaining 5 ingredients in a jar; cover tightly, and shake vigorously; pour over vegetables, stirring gently. Cover and chill at least 2 hours.

Serve with a slotted spoon.

Per Serving:

Calories 54	Fiber 1.8g
Fat 0.3g (sat 0.0g)	Cholesterol 0mg
Protein 2.9g	Sodium 79mg
Carbohydrate 11.2g	Exchange: 1 Starch

Make Ahead!

Mexican Corn Salad

Yield: 2 (²/₃-cup) servings

1	(8¾-ounce) can no-salt-added whole-kernel corn, drained
¼	cup chopped cucumber
¼	cup seeded, chopped tomato
1	tablespoon chopped green onions
¾	teaspoon seeded, minced jalapeño pepper
2	teaspoons fresh lime juice
½	teaspoon vegetable oil
⅛	teaspoon ground cumin

Dash of salt
Dash of pepper

Combine first 5 ingredients in a medium bowl; toss well. Combine lime juice and remaining 4 ingredients, stirring with a wire whisk. Pour lime juice mixture over vegetable mixture, and toss well. Cover and chill at least 2 hours.

Stir just before serving.

Per Serving:

Calories 73	Fiber 0.8g
Fat 1.9g (sat 0.2g)	Cholesterol 0mg
Protein 1.8g	Sodium 77mg
Carbohydrate 12.6g	Exchanges: 1 Starch, ½ Fat

This jalapeño-hot corn side dish is great served with Tex-Mex entrées like burritos and enchiladas.

Make Ahead!

Confetti Rice Salad

Yield: 5 (1-cup) servings

1	(10½-ounce) can low-sodium chicken broth
1	cup water
1	cup long-grain rice, uncooked
½	cup chopped carrot
¼	cup lemon juice
1	tablespoon olive oil
¾	cup seeded, chopped plum tomato (about 2 medium)
¾	cup chopped cooked reduced-fat, low-salt ham
⅓	cup freshly grated Parmesan cheese
⅓	cup sliced green onions
⅓	cup chopped fresh parsley

Combine broth and water in a large saucepan; bring to a boil. Add rice and carrot; stir well. Reduce heat to low; cover and simmer 20 minutes or until liquid is absorbed and rice is tender.

Add lemon juice and oil to rice mixture; stir well. Add tomato and remaining ingredients; toss well. Transfer to a serving bowl. Cover and chill at least 2 hours.

Stir just before serving.

Per Serving:

Calories 244	Fiber 1.5g
Fat 6.6g (sat 2.5g)	Cholesterol 17mg
Protein 10.9g	Sodium 339mg
Carbohydrate 35.4g	Exchanges: 2 Starch, 1 Vegetable, 1 Fat

Tabbouleh

Yield: 8 (¾-cup) servings

1	cup bulgur (or cracked wheat), uncooked
2	cups boiling water
1	large tomato, unpeeled and chopped
1	cup minced fresh parsley
1	green onion, chopped
2	tablespoons minced fresh mint leaves
¼	cup lemon juice
1	tablespoon olive oil
¼	teaspoon salt
¼	teaspoon pepper

Combine bulgur and water; let stand 1 hour. Drain bulgur. Add tomato and next 3 ingredients to bulgur; toss well.

Combine lemon juice and remaining 3 ingredients; pour over bulgur mixture, and toss well. Cover and chill 8 hours.

Stir just before serving.

Per Serving:

Calories 85

Fat 2.1g (sat 0.3g)

Protein 2.7g

Carbohydrate 15.6g

Fiber 3.8g

Cholesterol 0mg

Sodium 82mg

Exchange: 1 Starch

Tabbouleh (tuh-BOO-luh) is a traditional Middle Eastern bulgur salad. There are many variations, but the key ingredients are always bulgur, chopped tomato, onions, parsley or mint, lemon juice, and olive oil.

Jalapeño Potato Salad

Yield: 6 (½-cup) servings

4	medium-size round red potatoes (about 1 pound)
2	tablespoons finely chopped green onions
2	tablespoons minced fresh cilantro
¼	cup low-fat sour cream
2	tablespoons nonfat mayonnaise
2	teaspoons Dijon mustard
2	teaspoons seeded, minced jalapeño pepper
½	teaspoon pepper
¼	teaspoon salt

Wash potatoes. Cook in boiling water to cover 20 to 25 minutes or until tender; drain and cool slightly. Coarsely chop potatoes, and place in a medium bowl.

Combine onions and remaining 7 ingredients in a small bowl, stirring well. Spoon mixture over potato, and toss gently. Cover and chill at least 3 hours.

Per Serving:

Calories 76	Fiber 1.6g
Fat 1.4g (sat 0.8g)	Cholesterol 4mg
Protein 2.1g	Sodium 222mg
Carbohydrate 14.1g	Exchange: 1 Starch

This potato salad will add punch to a meal featuring a mildly flavored meat or sandwich.

Garden Pasta Salad

Yield: 6 (1-cup) servings

6   ounces corkscrew pasta, uncooked
3   cups peeled, seeded, and coarsely chopped tomato (about
       3 medium)
1   cup peeled, seeded, and chopped cucumber (about 1 medium)
¼   cup chopped green pepper
¼   cup chopped fresh parsley
2   tablespoons sliced green onions
⅓   cup fat-free Italian dressing
Dash of hot sauce
¾   cup crumbled feta cheese
Chopped fresh parsley (optional)

Cook pasta according to package directions, omitting salt and fat. Drain; set aside.

Combine tomato and next 4 ingredients in a large bowl. Combine dressing and hot sauce, stirring well.

Add pasta and dressing mixture to vegetable mixture, and toss. Cover and chill at least 30 minutes.

Sprinkle cheese evenly over salad just before serving. Garnish with chopped parsley, if desired.

Per Serving:

Calories 173

Fat 3.8g (sat 2.2g)

Protein 6.7g

Carbohydrate 28.5g

Fiber 2.1g

Cholesterol 13mg

Sodium 313mg

Exchanges: 2 Starch, 1 Fat

Make Ahead!

Fruited Chicken Salad

Yield: 5 (1-cup) servings

3	cups chopped cooked chicken breast
1	cup chopped celery
¼	cup minced onion
2	tablespoons lemon juice
¼	teaspoon salt
⅛	teaspoon pepper
1	(8-ounce) can pineapple chunks in juice, drained
1	cup seedless green grapes, halved
⅓	cup reduced-fat mayonnaise
3	tablespoons slivered almonds, toasted

Lettuce leaves

Combine first 6 ingredients; cover and chill at least 3 hours.

To serve, add pineapple, grapes, mayonnaise, and almonds to chicken mixture; toss well. Serve on lettuce leaves.

Per Serving:

Calories 277	Fiber 2.0g
Fat 10.3g (sat 1.9g)	Cholesterol 84mg
Protein 30.7g	Sodium 331mg
Carbohydrate 15.0g	Exchanges: 1 Fruit, 4 Very Lean Meat, 1 Fat

Microwave 1½ pounds raw skinned, boned chicken breast halves at HIGH for about 8 minutes to get 3 cups chopped chicken. Or look for cooked diced chicken in the freezer section of your grocery store.

Grilled Chicken Caesar Salad

Yield: 6 (2-cup) servings

4   (4-ounce) skinned, boned chicken breast halves
½   cup reduced-fat Caesar dressing, divided
2   cups cubed French bread
Olive oil-flavored cooking spray
6   cups torn romaine lettuce
1   cup sliced cucumber
2   medium tomatoes, each cut into 8 wedges
2   tablespoons freshly grated Parmesan cheese
Freshly ground pepper (optional)

Place chicken in a heavy-duty, zip-top plastic bag; pour ¼ cup dressing over chicken. Seal bag, and shake until chicken is well coated. Marinate in refrigerator 1 hour, turning bag once.

Coat French bread cubes with cooking spray; place in a single layer on a baking sheet. Bake at 350° for 10 minutes or until lightly browned.

Remove chicken from marinade, discarding marinade. Coat grill rack with cooking spray; place on grill over medium-hot coals (350° to 400°). Place chicken on rack; grill, covered, 5 minutes on each side or until done. Cut chicken into slices.

Combine chicken, bread cubes, lettuce, and next 3 ingredients in a large serving bowl. Pour remaining ¼ cup dressing over lettuce mixture, and toss well. Sprinkle with pepper, if desired.

Per Serving:

Calories 206	Fiber 1.7g
Fat 7.2g (sat 1.3g)	Cholesterol 53mg
Protein 20.5g	Sodium 554mg
Carbohydrate 13.0g	Exchanges: 1 Starch, 2½ Lean Meat

(Photograph on page 139)

Taco Salad Supreme

Yield: 6 servings

3   (6-inch) corn tortillas
Cooking spray
½   pound freshly ground raw turkey
1   cup chopped onion
1   cup frozen whole-kernel corn, thawed
2   tablespoons minced jalapeño pepper
2   teaspoons chili powder
1   (15-ounce) can no-salt-added black beans, rinsed and drained
8   cups thinly sliced romaine lettuce leaves
¼   cup reduced-fat olive oil vinaigrette
1   cup (4 ounces) shredded reduced-fat Cheddar cheese
1   cup seeded, chopped tomato (about 1 medium)
¼   cup minced fresh cilantro
2   tablespoons sliced ripe olives
½   cup nonfat sour cream

Coat tortillas with cooking spray; cut into strips. Place on a baking sheet; bake at 400° for 15 minutes.

Coat a nonstick skillet with cooking spray; place over medium heat until hot. Add turkey and next 3 ingredients; cook over medium heat until turkey is done, stirring until it crumbles. Stir in chili powder and beans; cook until thoroughly heated.

Combine lettuce and vinaigrette. Place 2 cups lettuce mixture on each of 6 plates. Spoon turkey mixture over lettuce. Top evenly with cheese and remaining 4 ingredients; serve with tortilla strips.

Per Serving:

Calories 274	Fiber 5.5g
Fat 8.4g (sat 2.9g)	Cholesterol 37mg
Protein 22.1g	Sodium 337mg
Carbohydrate 29.5g	Exchanges: 2 Starch, 2 Medium-Fat Meat

Grilled Salmon on Greens

Yield: 4 servings

1¼   pounds medium-size round red potatoes, quartered
¾   pound fresh green beans, trimmed
1   tablespoon lemon juice
2   teaspoons low-sodium Worcestershire sauce
1   teaspoon olive oil
1   pound salmon fillets
Cooking spray
½   cup reduced-fat olive oil vinaigrette
¼   cup sliced ripe olives
8   cups mixed salad greens

Cook potato in a saucepan in boiling water to cover 12 minutes or just until tender. Drain. Cook beans in saucepan in boiling water 5 minutes or until crisp-tender; drain. Cut beans in half crosswise.

Combine lemon juice, Worcestershire sauce, and oil; brush on fish. Coat grill rack with cooking spray; place on grill over medium-hot coals (350° to 400°). Place fish and potato on rack; grill, covered, 6 minutes on each side or until fish flakes easily when tested with a fork. Remove fish and potato from grill. Flake fish into chunks with a fork.

Combine fish, potato, beans, vinaigrette, and olives; spoon over greens.

Per Serving:

Calories 415	Fiber 5.5g
Fat 18.3g (sat 2.1g)	Cholesterol 77mg
Protein 29.7g	Sodium 404mg
Carbohydrate 35.2g	Exchanges: 2 Starch, 1 Vegetable, 3 Medium-Fat Meat, 1 Fat

Sides

Asparagus with Mock Hollandaise Sauce, page 162

Asparagus with Mock Hollandaise Sauce • Broccoli-Cheese Casserole • Seasoned Green Beans • Orange-Glazed Carrots Crispy Oven-Fried Okra • Cheesy Squash Casserole Simple Sesame Spinach • Roasted-Garlic Mashed Potatoes Roasted New Potatoes • Orange Sweet Potatoes • Zippy Garlic-Cheese Grits • Spicy Mexican Rice • Macaroni and Cheese • Linguine with Red Pepper Sauce • Garlic-Lemon Pasta

Asparagus with Mock Hollandaise Sauce

Yield: 8 servings

1	pound fresh asparagus
2	egg yolks
1	cup water
2	tablespoons cornstarch
½	teaspoon salt
2	tablespoons lemon juice
1	tablespoon margarine

Lemon zest (optional)

Snap off tough ends of asparagus. Cook asparagus, covered, in a small amount of boiling water 8 to 10 minutes or until tender; drain. Set aside, and keep warm.

Place egg yolks in a small bowl; stir well with a wire whisk.

Combine water, cornstarch, and salt in a small, heavy saucepan. Cook over low heat, stirring constantly, until mixture comes to a boil and begins to thicken. Remove from heat; add 2 tablespoons cornstarch mixture to egg yolks, stirring constantly with a wire whisk. Add egg yolk mixture to remaining cornstarch mixture; cook, stirring constantly, 2 minutes or until temperature reaches 160°. Remove from heat; stir in lemon juice and margarine.

To serve, spoon sauce over asparagus, and sprinkle with lemon zest, if desired.

Per Serving:

Calories 49	Fiber 1.0g
Fat 3.0g (sat 1.0g)	Cholesterol 53mg
Protein 2.0g	Sodium 167mg
Carbohydrate 4.0g	Exchanges: 1 Vegetable, ½ Fat

(Photograph on page 161)

Broccoli-Cheese Casserole

Yield: 8 servings

2   (10-ounce) packages frozen broccoli spears
Butter-flavored cooking spray
1   cup (4 ounces) shredded reduced-fat sharp Cheddar cheese
½   cup fat-free egg substitute
½   cup nonfat mayonnaise
½   cup finely chopped onion
1   (10¾-ounce) can reduced-fat, reduced-sodium cream
        of mushroom soup
1   (6-ounce) box reduced-sodium chicken-flavored stuffing mix

Cook broccoli according to package directions; drain. Arrange broccoli in an 11- x 7- x 1½-inch baking dish coated with cooking spray. Sprinkle with cheese. Combine egg substitute and next 3 ingredients; spread over cheese.

Combine ¾ cup stuffing mix and 2½ teaspoons of the mix's seasoning packet, tossing well. Sprinkle over casserole; coat with cooking spray. (Reserve remaining stuffing mix and seasoning packet for another use.)

Bake at 350° for 30 minutes or until thoroughly heated. Serve warm.

Per Serving:

Calories 134	Fiber 1.7g
Fat 4.1g (sat 1.9g)	Cholesterol 13mg
Protein 8.9g	Sodium 537mg
Carbohydrate 16.1g	Exchanges: 1 Starch, 1 Fat

The seasoned stuffing mix makes a crunchy topping for the creamy broccoli mixture.

Seasoned Green Beans

Yield: 4 servings

1	pound fresh green beans
1¾	cups peeled, seeded, and coarsely chopped tomato (about 2 medium)
⅓	cup canned no-salt-added beef broth
1	teaspoon minced garlic
2	ounces reduced-fat, low-salt ham, diced
2	tablespoons chopped fresh parsley
1	teaspoon dried thyme
¼	teaspoon pepper

Trim stem end from beans. Arrange beans in a steamer basket over boiling water; cover and steam 10 minutes.

Combine tomato and next 3 ingredients in a large saucepan. Cook, uncovered, over medium heat 3 minutes, stirring often. Stir in beans, parsley, thyme, and pepper. Cover and cook over low heat 10 minutes or until beans are tender.

Serve immediately.

Per Serving:

Calories 74	Fiber 3.4g
Fat 1.1g (sat 0.3g)	Cholesterol 7mg
Protein 5.4g	Sodium 126mg
Carbohydrate 12.8g	Exchanges: 2 Vegetable

When you season fresh beans with lean
ham instead of ham hock, you get all of
the flavor, but none of the fat.

Orange-Glazed Carrots

Yield: 4 (½-cup) servings

1	pound carrots, scraped and cut into ¼-inch-thick slices
¾	cup fat-free, reduced-sodium chicken broth
2	tablespoons frozen orange juice concentrate
2	teaspoons granulated sugar substitute (such as Sugar Twin)
¼	teaspoon ground ginger

Combine carrot and broth in a medium saucepan; bring to a boil. Cover, reduce heat, and simmer 10 minutes.

Add orange juice concentrate, sugar substitute, and ginger to carrot mixture, stirring well. Cook, uncovered, over medium heat 8 minutes or until carrot is tender and liquid is reduced, stirring occasionally.

Serve immediately.

Per Serving:

Calories 69	Fiber 3.3g
Fat 0.2g (sat 0.0g)	Cholesterol 0mg
Protein 1.3g	Sodium 36mg
Carbohydrate 16.0g	Exchanges: ½ Fruit, 2 Vegetable

Crispy Oven-Fried Okra

Yield: 12 (½-cup) servings

1¾ pounds fresh okra
1½ cups yellow cornmeal
½ teaspoon salt
⅛ teaspoon pepper
½ cup nonfat buttermilk
1 large egg, lightly beaten
Cooking spray

Wash okra; trim ends, and cut into ½-inch pieces. Combine cornmeal, salt, and pepper in a medium bowl; stir well, and set aside.

Combine buttermilk and egg in a large bowl; stir in okra. Let stand 10 minutes.

Remove okra with a slotted spoon; discard remaining buttermilk mixture. Combine okra and cornmeal mixture, tossing to coat okra well. Place okra on a baking sheet coated with cooking spray. Bake at 450° for 40 minutes or until crisp, stirring occasionally.

Serve immediately.

Per Serving:

Calories 84	Fiber 2.1g
Fat 1.1g (sat 0.3g)	Cholesterol 19mg
Protein 3.1g	Sodium 123mg
Carbohydrate 15.9g	Exchange: 1 Starch

Cheesy Squash Casserole

Yield: 8 servings

2   pounds yellow squash, sliced
¾   cup chopped onion
1   tablespoon reduced-calorie margarine
2   tablespoons all-purpose flour
1   cup fat-free milk
¾   cup (3 ounces) shredded reduced-fat Cheddar cheese
½   teaspoon salt
¼   teaspoon pepper
Cooking spray
½   cup soft breadcrumbs, toasted

Cook squash and onion in a small amount of boiling water 10 to 12 minutes or until vegetables are tender. Drain; set aside.

Melt margarine in a medium-size, heavy saucepan over medium heat. Add flour; cook, stirring constantly, 1 minute. Gradually add milk; cook, stirring constantly, until mixture is thickened and bubbly. Remove from heat; add cheese, salt, and pepper, stirring until cheese melts. Add squash mixture; stir well.

Spoon squash mixture into a shallow 1½-quart baking dish coated with cooking spray. Sprinkle squash mixture evenly with breadcrumbs. Bake at 350° for 20 to 25 minutes or until mixture is thoroughly heated.

Serve immediately.

Per Serving:

Calories 95	Fiber 2.2g
Fat 3.4g (sat 1.4g)	Cholesterol 8mg
Protein 6.2g	Sodium 277mg
Carbohydrate 11.0g	Exchanges: 2 Vegetable, ½ Fat

Simple Sesame Spinach

Yield: 4 (½-cup) servings

1 pound fresh spinach
Cooking spray
1 tablespoon sesame seeds, toasted
1 teaspoon lemon juice
¼ teaspoon salt

Wash spinach thoroughly; remove and discard stems from spinach. Tear into bite-size pieces.

Coat a Dutch oven with cooking spray; place over medium heat until hot. Add spinach; cover and cook 3 minutes or until spinach wilts, stirring occasionally. Remove from heat, and stir in sesame seeds, lemon juice, and salt, tossing gently.

Serve immediately.

Per Serving:

Calories 46	Fiber 4.2g
Fat 2.5g (sat 0.3g)	Cholesterol 0mg
Protein 3.9g	Sodium 229mg
Carbohydrate 4.0g	Exchanges: 1 Vegetable, ½ Fat

To toast sesame seeds, place them in a hot nonstick skillet over medium-high heat (no oil) for 3 to 4 minutes, stirring constantly. Don't cook them much longer, or they'll burn.

Roasted-Garlic Mashed Potatoes

Yield: 8 (½-cup) servings

2	heads garlic
1	teaspoon olive oil
2	pounds baking potatoes, peeled and cut into 1-inch pieces
⅓	cup fat-free milk
1½	tablespoons reduced-calorie margarine
½	teaspoon salt
¼	teaspoon pepper

Remove papery husks from garlic. Place garlic on a square of aluminum foil; drizzle with oil, and wrap in foil. Bake at 425° for 30 minutes; set aside.

Place potato in a medium saucepan; add water to cover. Bring to a boil; reduce heat. Cook, uncovered, 15 to 20 minutes or until tender; drain. Mash potato with a potato masher. Add milk and remaining 3 ingredients; mash until fluffy.

Cut off ends of garlic; squeeze pulp from cloves into potato mixture, and stir.

Serve immediately.

Per Serving:

Calories 120	Fiber 1.6g
Fat 2.1g (sat 0.3g)	Cholesterol 0mg
Protein 2.9g	Sodium 180mg
Carbohydrate 23.5g	Exchanges: 1½ Starch

Roasted New Potatoes

Yield: 8 servings (serving size: 3 potatoes)

24   small round red potatoes (about 2⅓ pounds)
Olive oil-flavored cooking spray
¼   cup Italian-seasoned breadcrumbs
¼   cup freshly grated Parmesan cheese
¾   teaspoon paprika

Place potatoes in a Dutch oven; add water to cover. Bring to a boil; reduce heat, and cook, uncovered, 15 minutes or until tender; drain and cool slightly.

Quarter potatoes; coat with cooking spray. Combine breadcrumbs, cheese, and paprika; sprinkle over wedges, tossing to coat well. Arrange in a single layer on a baking sheet coated with cooking spray. Bake at 450° for 20 to 25 minutes or until coating is crispy.

Serve immediately.

Per Serving:

Calories 117	Fiber 2.4g
Fat 1.3g (sat 0.7g)	Cholesterol 2mg
Protein 4.3g	Sodium 91mg
Carbohydrate 22.8g	Exchanges: 1½ Starch

Enjoy these crispy Parmesan cheese-coated potatoes instead of high-fat French fries.

Orange Sweet Potatoes

Yield: 8 servings

3	medium-size sweet potatoes (about 2 pounds)
⅔	cup orange juice
1	tablespoon reduced-calorie margarine, melted
¼	teaspoon ground cinnamon

Peel sweet potatoes, and cut lengthwise into ¼-inch-thick slices. Arrange potato slices in a single layer in a 13- x 9- x 2-inch baking dish.

Combine orange juice, margarine, and cinnamon in a small bowl, stirring well. Pour over sweet potato slices. Bake, uncovered, at 400° for 30 minutes or until tender, turning once.

Serve immediately.

Per Serving:

Calories 129	Fiber 3.3g
Fat 1.2g (sat 0.2g)	Cholesterol 0mg
Protein 1.9g	Sodium 28mg
Carbohydrate 28.3g	Exchanges: 1 Starch, 1 Fruit

Zippy Garlic-Cheese Grits

Yield: 10 (½-cup) servings

4	cups water
½	cup fat-free milk
1	cup quick-cooking grits, uncooked
2	teaspoons low-sodium Worcestershire sauce
1	teaspoon minced garlic
¼	teaspoon salt
¼	teaspoon hot sauce
1½	cups (6 ounces) shredded reduced-fat Cheddar cheese

Combine water and milk in a medium saucepan; bring to a boil. Stir in grits and next 4 ingredients. Cover, reduce heat, and simmer 5 to 7 minutes or until creamy, stirring occasionally.

Stir in cheese. Cook, uncovered, over medium heat until cheese melts and grits are thickened, stirring often.

Serve immediately.

Per Serving:

Calories 111	Fiber 0.8g
Fat 3.3g (sat 1.9g)	Cholesterol 11mg
Protein 6.9g	Sodium 196mg
Carbohydrate 13.4g	Exchanges: 1 Starch, ½ Medium-Fat Meat

Spicy Mexican Rice

Yield: 10 (½-cup) servings

Cooking spray
1½ teaspoons vegetable oil
1 cup long-grain rice, uncooked
1 cup chopped onion
2 cups water
2 cups chopped tomato
⅔ cup chopped green pepper
2 teaspoons beef-flavored bouillon granules
1 teaspoon chili powder
½ teaspoon garlic powder
½ teaspoon ground red pepper
Fresh cilantro sprigs (optional)

Coat a large saucepan with cooking spray; add oil. Place over medium heat until hot. Add rice and onion; cook 3 minutes, stirring occasionally. Add water and next 6 ingredients; bring to a boil. Cover, reduce heat, and simmer 25 minutes or until liquid is absorbed and rice is tender.

Transfer to a bowl; garnish with cilantro sprigs, if desired.

Per Serving:

Calories 93	Fiber 1.2g
Fat 1.3g (sat 0.3g)	Cholesterol 0mg
Protein 2.0g	Sodium 197mg
Carbohydrate 18.6g	Exchange: 1 Starch

Macaroni and Cheese

Yield: 11 (½-cup) servings

1	(8-ounce) package elbow macaroni
2	tablespoons reduced-calorie margarine
2	tablespoons all-purpose flour
2	cups fat-free milk
1½	cups (6 ounces) shredded reduced-fat sharp Cheddar cheese
½	teaspoon salt
3	tablespoons fat-free egg substitute
Cooking spray	
¼	teaspoon paprika

Cook pasta according to package directions, omitting salt and fat.

Melt margarine in a heavy saucepan over low heat; add flour, stirring until smooth. Cook, stirring constantly, 1 minute. Gradually add milk; cook over medium heat, stirring constantly, until thickened and bubbly. Add cheese and salt, stirring until cheese melts. Gradually stir about one-fourth cheese mixture into egg substitute. Add egg substitute mixture to remaining cheese mixture, stirring constantly.

Combine cheese sauce and pasta; pour into a 2-quart baking dish coated with cooking spray. Sprinkle with paprika. Bake at 350° for 25 to 30 minutes or until thoroughly heated.

Serve immediately.

Per Serving:

Calories 111	Fiber 0.4g
Fat 4.6g (sat 2.0g)	Cholesterol 11mg
Protein 7.6g	Sodium 268mg
Carbohydrate 9.8g	Exchanges: 1 Starch, 1 Fat

Linguine with Red Pepper Sauce

Yield: 6 (½-cup) servings

Cooking spray
1   teaspoon olive oil
1½   cups chopped sweet red pepper
1   clove garlic, crushed
2   tablespoons chopped fresh basil
2   tablespoons balsamic vinegar
⅛   teaspoon salt
⅛   teaspoon black pepper
6   ounces linguine, uncooked
Fresh basil sprigs (optional)

Coat a nonstick skillet with cooking spray; add oil. Place over medium heat until hot. Add sweet red pepper and garlic; cook, uncovered, 30 minutes, stirring occasionally. Set aside, and cool slightly.

Place pepper mixture in container of an electric blender or food processor; add chopped basil and next 3 ingredients. Cover and process until smooth, stopping once to scrape down sides.

Cook pasta according to package directions, omitting salt and fat.

To serve, top pasta with pepper sauce. Garnish with basil sprigs, if desired.

Per Serving:

Calories 117	Fiber 1.7g
Fat 1.5g (sat 0.2g)	Cholesterol 0mg
Protein 3.7g	Sodium 51mg
Carbohydrate 22.2g	Exchanges: 1 Starch, 1 Vegetable

Garlic-Lemon Pasta

Yield: 5 (½-cup) servings

5	ounces angel hair pasta, uncooked
1½	tablespoons reduced-calorie margarine
¼	cup grated Parmesan cheese
2	tablespoons lemon juice
½	teaspoon pepper
2	cloves garlic, crushed

Cook pasta according to package directions, omitting salt and fat.

Melt margarine in a small saucepan over medium heat; stir in Parmesan cheese and remaining 3 ingredients. Pour over pasta; toss gently.

Serve immediately.

Per Serving:

Calories 80

Fat 3.6g (sat 1.1g)

Protein 3.1g

Carbohydrate 9.2g

Fiber 0.5g

Cholesterol 3mg

Sodium 108mg

Exchanges: 1 Starch, 1 Fat

Soups & Sandwiches

Club Sandwiches, page 193

Black Bean Soup • Minestrone • Jambalaya Stew • Chicken
Divan Soup • Spinach-Chicken Noodle Soup • Wagon Wheel Beef
Soup • Seafood Gumbo • Hearty Sausage-Bean Chili • Grilled
Cheese Sandwiches • Club Sandwiches • Spicy Chicken Pockets
Marinated Chicken Sandwiches • Sausage-Pepper Buns

Black Bean Soup

Yield: 8 (1-cup) servings

3	(15-ounce) cans no-salt-added black beans, drained
2	(14¼-ounce) cans fat-free, reduced-sodium chicken broth
1	cup chopped onion (about 1 medium)
1	cup chopped sweet red pepper (about 1 medium)
2	cloves garlic, minced
½	pound extra-lean cooked ham, diced
¾	teaspoon dried oregano
½	teaspoon black pepper
¼	teaspoon salt

Combine first 5 ingredients in a Dutch oven; bring to a boil. Cover, reduce heat, and simmer 30 minutes.

Transfer 2 cups bean mixture to container of an electric blender or food processor; cover and process until smooth, stopping once to scrape down sides. Return pureed bean mixture to Dutch oven. Add ham and remaining ingredients. Bring to a boil; reduce heat, and simmer, uncovered, 20 minutes or until thickened.

Remove from heat, and serve immediately.

Per Serving:

Calories 164	Fiber 3.9g
Fat 2.1g (sat 0.6g)	Cholesterol 15mg
Protein 13.4g	Sodium 418mg
Carbohydrate 22.2g	Exchanges: 1½ Starch, 1 Lean Meat

Minestrone

Yield: 7 (1½-cup) servings

Cooking spray
1   (10-ounce) package frozen chopped onion, celery, and
         pepper blend, thawed
4   (14¼-ounce) cans no-salt-added beef broth
1   (16-ounce) package frozen vegetables with zucchini,
         cauliflower, carrots, and beans, thawed
1   (14½-ounce) can Italian-style tomatoes, undrained and chopped
½   teaspoon dried basil
¼   teaspoon salt
¼   teaspoon pepper
1   cup small pasta shells, uncooked
¼   cup plus 3 tablespoons freshly grated Parmesan cheese

Coat a Dutch oven with cooking spray; place over medium-high heat until hot. Add chopped onion blend; sauté 5 minutes. Add broth and next 5 ingredients. Bring to a boil; cover, reduce heat, and simmer 30 minutes.

Add pasta to Dutch oven; simmer 15 minutes or until pasta is tender.

Spoon evenly into 7 bowls; sprinkle each serving with 1 tablespoon cheese, and serve immediately.

Per Serving:

Calories 136	Fiber 3.0g
Fat 1.5g (sat 0.8g)	Cholesterol 3mg
Protein 6.7g	Sodium 477mg
Carbohydrate 21.5g	Exchanges: 1 Starch, 1 Vegetable

Ready in 15 Minutes!

Jambalaya Stew

Yield: 16 (1-cup) servings

4	cups water
2½	cups chopped tomato (about 2 large)
1½	cups chopped green pepper (about 2 small)
1	cup chopped onion (about 1 medium)
1	teaspoon dried Italian seasoning
1	teaspoon chili powder
1	teaspoon hot sauce
¾	teaspoon salt
3	cloves garlic, minced
1	bay leaf
2	cups instant rice, uncooked
3	(8-ounce) cans no-salt-added tomato sauce
2	(15-ounce) cans no-salt-added red kidney beans, undrained
1	(16-ounce) package frozen sliced okra, thawed

Combine first 10 ingredients in a large Dutch oven. Bring to a boil; reduce heat, and cook, uncovered, 5 minutes. Add rice and remaining ingredients. Bring to a boil; reduce heat, and cook, uncovered, 5 minutes or until okra is tender.

Remove and discard bay leaf, and serve immediately.

Per Serving:

Calories 151

Fat 0.6g (sat 0.1g)

Protein 7.0g

Carbohydrate 30.7g

Fiber 3.2g

Cholesterol 0mg

Sodium 129mg

Exchanges: 2 Starch

Ready in 30 Minutes!

Chicken Divan Soup

Yield: 6 (1½-cup) servings

Cooking spray
1¼ pounds skinned, boned chicken breasts, cut into bite-size pieces
¾ cup chopped onion
2 cloves garlic, minced
1 cup cooked long-grain rice (cooked without salt or fat)
½ teaspoon pepper
¼ teaspoon salt
2 (4-ounce) cans sliced mushrooms, drained
1 (16-ounce) package frozen chopped broccoli, thawed
1 (14¼-ounce) can fat-free, reduced-sodium chicken broth
1 (12-ounce) can evaporated fat-free milk
1 (10¾-ounce) can reduced-fat, reduced-sodium cream of
     chicken soup

Coat a Dutch oven with cooking spray; place over medium-high heat until hot. Add chicken, onion, and garlic; sauté until onion is tender. Add rice and remaining ingredients, stirring well. Bring to a boil; cover, reduce heat, and simmer 15 minutes.

Remove from heat, and serve immediately.

Per Serving:

Calories 264

Fat 2.8g (sat 0.8g)

Protein 31.2g

Carbohydrate 26.7g

Fiber 2.4g

Cholesterol 61mg

Sodium 591mg

Exchanges: 1½ Starch, 1 Vegetable, 3 Very Lean Meat

Spinach-Chicken Noodle Soup

Yield: 8 (1 ½-cup) servings

4	(14¼-ounce) cans fat-free, reduced-sodium chicken broth
1	cup chopped onion (about 1 medium)
1	cup sliced carrot
2	(10¾-ounce) cans reduced-fat, reduced-sodium cream of chicken soup
1	(10-ounce) package frozen chopped spinach, thawed
4	cups chopped cooked chicken (skinned before cooking and cooked without salt)
2	cups medium egg noodles, uncooked
½	teaspoon salt
½	teaspoon pepper

Combine first 3 ingredients in a Dutch oven. Bring to a boil; cover, reduce heat, and simmer 15 minutes. Add canned soup and remaining ingredients. Bring to a boil; reduce heat, and simmer, uncovered, 15 minutes.

Remove from heat, and serve immediately.

Per Serving:

Calories 227	Fiber 2.3g
Fat 5.9g (sat 1.7g)	Cholesterol 71mg
Protein 22.0g	Sodium 388mg
Carbohydrate 18.9g	Exchanges: 1 Starch, 1 Vegetable, 2 Lean Meat

During the holidays, use your leftover turkey instead of chicken in this soup.

Wagon Wheel Beef Soup

Yield: 10 (1-cup) servings

Cooking spray
¾ pound ground round
1 cup chopped onion (about 1 medium)
3 cups cooked wagon wheel pasta (cooked without salt or fat)
3 cups low-fat spaghetti sauce
½ teaspoon ground oregano
2 (14¼-ounce) cans no-salt-added beef broth
1 (15-ounce) can no-salt-added kidney beans, undrained

Coat a Dutch oven with cooking spray; place over medium-high heat until hot. Add meat and onion; cook over medium heat until meat is browned, stirring until it crumbles. Drain.

Return meat mixture to Dutch oven; add cooked pasta and remaining ingredients. Cook 10 minutes or until thoroughly heated.

Remove from heat, and serve immediately.

Per Serving:

Calories 223	Fiber 2.4g
Fat 4.2g (sat 1.1g)	Cholesterol 29mg
Protein 17.1g	Sodium 261mg
Carbohydrate 29.2g	Exchanges: 2 Starch, 1½ Lean Meat

Seafood Gumbo

Yield: 8 (2-cup) servings

¼	cup plus 2 tablespoons all-purpose flour
4	(14½-ounce) cans no-salt-added stewed tomatoes, undrained
3	cups water
1	tablespoon salt-free Creole seasoning
¼	teaspoon pepper
1	(16-ounce) package frozen vegetable gumbo mixture
2	pounds medium-size peeled and deveined fresh shrimp
1	(15½-ounce) container fresh Standard oysters, drained

Sprinkle flour in a baking pan (Step 1). Bake at 400° for 10 minutes or until caramel colored, stirring every 5 minutes (Step 2).

Combine browned flour, tomatoes, and next 3 ingredients in a Dutch oven; stir. Bring to a boil; cover, reduce heat, and simmer 15 minutes. Add vegetables; cover and cook 20 minutes. Add shrimp and oysters; cook 5 minutes or until shrimp turn pink. Remove from heat, and serve immediately.

Per Serving:

Calories 257	Fiber 2.0g
Fat 3.1g (sat 0.7g)	Cholesterol 188mg
Protein 28.8g	Sodium 418mg
Carbohydrate 28.2g	Exchanges: 2 Starch, 3 Very Lean Meat

Browning Flour

Step 1

Step 2

Hearty Sausage-Bean Chili

Yield: 7 (1½-cup) servings

1	pound turkey breakfast sausage
¾	pound ground round
1½	cups frozen chopped onion, celery, and pepper blend, thawed
2	(15-ounce) cans no-salt-added dark red kidney beans, undrained
2	(14½-ounce) cans no-salt-added stewed tomatoes, undrained
1	(15-ounce) can no-salt-added pinto beans, undrained
1	(15-ounce) can chunky chili tomato sauce

Combine first 3 ingredients in a large Dutch oven. Place over medium-high heat, and cook until meat is browned, stirring until it crumbles. Drain and pat dry with paper towels. Wipe drippings from Dutch oven with a paper towel.

Return meat mixture to Dutch oven; add kidney beans and remaining ingredients. Bring to a boil; reduce heat, and simmer, uncovered, 20 minutes or until thickened, stirring occasionally.

Remove from heat, and serve immediately.

Per Serving:

Calories 298	Fiber 6.5g
Fat 8.5g (sat 1.9g)	Cholesterol 61mg
Protein 26.1g	Sodium 740mg
Carbohydrate 28.6g	Exchanges: 2 Starch, 3 Lean Meat

Look for turkey breakfast sausage in the refrigerator section with the other tubes of breakfast sausage or in the freezer section of the grocery store.

Ready in 15 Minutes!

Grilled Cheese Sandwiches

Yield: 4 servings

⅓ cup ⅓-less-fat cream cheese (Neufchâtel), softened
½ teaspoon dried basil
8 (1-ounce) slices white or whole wheat bread
4 (¾-ounce) slices fat-free sharp Cheddar cheese
4 (¾-ounce) slices fat-free mozzarella cheese
1 tablespoon plus 1 teaspoon reduced-calorie margarine, softened
Cooking spray

Combine cream cheese and basil, stirring well. Spread cream cheese mixture evenly over 1 side of each of 4 bread slices. Place Cheddar and mozzarella cheese slices over cream cheese mixture; top with remaining bread slices.

Spread margarine evenly over both sides of sandwiches. Place in a sandwich press or hot skillet coated with cooking spray. Cook 1 minute on each side or until bread is lightly browned and cheese melts.

Serve immediately.

Per Serving:

Calories 283

Fat 8.4g (sat 3.4g)

Protein 17.7g

Carbohydrate 33.7g

Fiber 1.1g

Cholesterol 22mg

Sodium 898mg

Exchanges: 2 Starch, 2 Very Lean Meat, 1 Fat

Club Sandwiches

Yield: 4 servings

¼   cup fat-free Thousand Island dressing
8   (1-ounce) slices whole wheat bread, toasted
4   green leaf lettuce leaves
8   slices tomato (about 2 medium)
4   ounces thinly sliced cooked turkey breast
4   (¾-ounce) slices fat-free sharp Cheddar cheese
4   slices turkey bacon, cooked and cut in half

Spread 1 tablespoon dressing over 1 side of each of 4 bread slices. Arrange lettuce and remaining 4 ingredients evenly on slices; top with remaining bread slices.

To serve, cut each sandwich into 4 triangles. Secure triangles with wooden picks.

Per Serving:

Calories 282	Fiber 3.3g
Fat 4.8g (sat 1.1g)	Cholesterol 34mg
Protein 21.9g	Sodium 982mg
Carbohydrate 38.2g	Exchanges: 2 Starch, 1 Vegetable, 2 Lean Meat

(Photograph on page 181)

Spicy Chicken Pockets

Yield: 8 servings

6   (4-ounce) skinned, boned chicken breast halves
3½   tablespoons salt-free Creole seasoning
1   tablespoon vegetable oil
Cooking spray
8   lettuce leaves
4   (6-inch) whole wheat pita bread rounds, cut in half crosswise
1   small purple onion, thinly sliced and separated into rings
1   cup alfalfa sprouts
¾   cup chopped cucumber
¾   cup chopped tomato

Rub both sides of chicken with Creole seasoning, and place in a large shallow dish. Cover and refrigerate at least 30 minutes.

Brush both sides of chicken evenly with oil. Coat grill rack with cooking spray; place on grill over medium-hot coals (350° to 400°). Place chicken on rack; grill, covered, 5 to 6 minutes on each side or until chicken is done.

Place 1 lettuce leaf in each pita half. Layer onion and remaining 3 ingredients evenly into pita halves. Cut chicken into strips, and arrange evenly over vegetables.

Serve warm.

Per Serving:

Calories 222	Fiber 4.0g
Fat 4.9g (sat 1.0g)	Cholesterol 54mg
Protein 22.3g	Sodium 217mg
Carbohydrate 19.6g	Exchanges: 1 Starch, 1 Vegetable, 2 Lean Meat

Marinated Chicken Sandwiches

Yield: 2 servings

2   (4-ounce) skinned, boned chicken breast halves
⅓   cup reduced-fat olive oil-balsamic vinaigrette
Cooking spray
2   teaspoons nonfat mayonnaise
2   teaspoons prepared mustard
2   whole wheat hamburger buns, split
2   green leaf lettuce leaves

Combine chicken and vinaigrette in a heavy-duty, zip-top plastic bag. Seal bag, and shake gently until chicken is coated. Marinate in refrigerator 8 hours, turning bag occasionally.

Remove chicken from marinade; discard marinade. Coat grill rack with cooking spray; place on grill over medium-hot coals (350° to 400°). Place chicken on rack; grill, covered, 5 to 6 minutes on each side or until done.

Combine mayonnaise and mustard; spread evenly over cut sides of bun halves. Place 1 lettuce leaf on bottom half of each bun; top with chicken and bun tops.

Serve warm.

Per Serving:

Calories 345	Fiber 1.9g
Fat 11.7g (sat 1.9g)	Cholesterol 90mg
Protein 31.5g	Sodium 678mg
Carbohydrate 28.5g	Exchanges: 2 Starch, 3½ Lean Meat

Sausage-Pepper Buns

Yield: 6 servings

Cooking spray
1 (14-ounce) package fat-free smoked turkey sausage, sliced
1 teaspoon reduced-calorie margarine
2 medium-size green peppers, seeded and sliced
1 large onion, sliced
1 teaspoon salt-free Greek seasoning
6 whole wheat hot dog buns

Coat a large nonstick skillet with cooking spray, and place over medium-high heat until hot. Add sausage, and cook 5 minutes or until browned, stirring often. Remove from skillet, and set aside. Wipe skillet dry with a paper towel.

Coat skillet with cooking spray, and add margarine. Place over medium-high heat until margarine melts. Add green pepper and onion; sauté 8 minutes or until vegetables are tender. Return sausage to skillet; sprinkle Greek seasoning over sausage. Cook 1 minute or until thoroughly heated, stirring occasionally.

Spoon sausage mixture evenly into buns.

Serve warm.

Per Serving:

Calories 249	Fiber 1.8g
Fat 4.5g (sat 0.7g)	Cholesterol 44mg
Protein 14.8g	Sodium 931mg
Carbohydrate 37.0g	Exchanges: 2 Starch, 1 Vegetable, 1 Medium-Fat Meat

7-DAY MENU PLANNER

Explanation of Menus

Use these menus and the recipes in the book to make your meal plan work for you. Since meal and snack plans differ according to dietary treatments and goals, this weekly menu planner is simply a guide to recipes and food items that make pleasing meals. Use your own meal plan to determine the number of servings you can have, or the number of other items you can add to your meal.

Page numbers are provided for you to refer to the recipes in the book. The other items are listed to round out the meal; substitute as desired. Start with this menu plan for ideas and then create your own meal plans using other recipes in the book.

Day 1

BREAKFAST
Oatmeal
Whole wheat toast with spreadable fruit
½ grapefruit
Fat-free milk

LUNCH
Grilled Chicken Caesar Salad (page 157)
Breadsticks
Green grapes

DINNER
Individual Meat Loaves (page 97)
Frozen mashed potatoes
Steamed green beans
Unsweetened applesauce

SNACK
Low-fat Cheddar cheese
Low-fat crackers

Day 2

BREAKFAST
Yogurt-Pecan Waffles (page 31)
Sugar-free maple syrup
Fresh strawberries
Fat-free milk

LUNCH
Grilled Cheese Sandwiches (page 192)
Canned reduced-sodium tomato soup
Apple wedges

DINNER
Cashew Chicken (page 123)
Spinach salad with low-fat dressing
Mini rice cakes

SNACK
Low-fat popcorn sprinkled with Parmesan cheese

Day 3

BREAKFAST
Bran flakes cereal
1 small banana
Fat-free milk

LUNCH
Taco Salad Supreme (page 159)
Fresh orange slices

DINNER
Beef Kabobs (page 99)
Rice
French bread

SNACK
½ turkey sandwich (made with 2 ounces turkey, mustard, and 1 slice bread)

Day 4

BREAKFAST
Blueberry Muffins (page 32)
Orange juice
Fat-free milk

LUNCH
Fruited Chicken Salad (page 156)
Carrot sticks
Tomato slices
Low-fat crackers

DINNER
Easy Parmesan Flounder (page 63)
Steamed new potatoes
Steamed broccoli spears
Whole wheat rolls

SNACK
Sugar-free hot chocolate
Graham crackers

Day 5

BREAKFAST
English muffins
Poached egg
Grapefruit juice

LUNCH
Club Sandwiches (page 193)
Colorful Coleslaw (page 146)
1 medium apple

DINNER
Spinach Lasagna (page 85)
Tossed salad with low-fat dressing
Sugar-free gelatin dessert

SNACK
Reduced-fat Swiss cheese
Pretzels

Day 6

BREAKFAST
Banana Bread (page 40)
Scrambled egg or egg substitute
Orange juice
Fat-free milk

LUNCH
Marinated Chicken Sandwiches (page 196)
Low-fat potato chips
Cantaloupe slices

DINNER
Easy Pork Parmesan (page 111)
Spaghetti or linguine noodles
Orange-Pecan Mixed Green Salad (page 143)

SNACK
Cheese toast (made with 1 ounce cheese and 1 slice whole wheat bread)

Day 7

BREAKFAST
Cinnamon French Toast (page 26)
Orange juice
Fat-free milk

LUNCH
Black Bean Soup (page 182)
Low-fat tortilla chips
Pineapple slices

DINNER
Three-Pepper Pizza (page 89)
Tossed salad with low-fat dressing
No-sugar-added ice cream

SNACK
Rice cakes
Peanut butter

Nutrition Notes

Delicious Ways to Control Diabetes gives you the nutrition facts you want to know. We provide the following information with every recipe.

values are for one serving of the recipe

Per Serving:

Calories 299

Fat 2.0g (sat 0.4g)

Protein 22.8g

Carbohydrate 29.1g

total carbohydrate in one serving

Fiber 2.0g

grams are abbreviated "g"

Cholesterol 47 mg

milligrams are abbreviated "mg"

Sodium 644mg

Exchanges: 2 Starch, 2 Medium-Fat Meat

exchange values are for one serving

Nutritional Analyses

The nutritional values used in our calculations either come from a computer program by Computrition, Inc., or are provided by food manufacturers. The values are based on the following assumptions:

- When we give a range for an ingredient, we calculate using the lesser amount.
- Only the amount of marinade absorbed is calculated.
- Garnishes and optional ingredients are not included in the analysis.

Diabetic Exchanges

Exchange values for all recipes are provided for people who use them for meal planning. The exchange values are based on the Exchange Lists for Meal Planning developed by the American Diabetes Association and The American Dietetic Association.

Carbohydrates

If you count carbohydrates, look for the value in the nutrient analysis. New American Diabetes Association guidelines loosen the restriction on sugar and encourage you to look at the total grams of carbohydrate in a serving. We have used small amounts of sugar in some recipes. We have also used a variety of sugar substitutes when the use of a substitute yields a quality product (see the Sugar Substitute Guide on page 10).

Sodium

Current dietary recommendations advise a daily sodium intake of 2,400 milligrams. We have limited the sodium in these recipes by using reduced-sodium products whenever possible.

If you must restrict sodium in your diet, please note the sodium value per serving and see if you should modify the recipe further.

Recipe Index

Appetizers
  Cheese
    Pineapple Cheese Ball, 18
    Swiss-Onion Dip, 15
  Dips
    Artichoke and Green Chile Dip, 16
    Black Bean Dip, 13
    Orange Dip, 14
    Swiss-Onion Dip, 15
  Pizza Bites, 19
  Salsa, Speedy, 12
Apples
  Salad, Fresh Fruit, 140
Applesauce-Bran Muffins, 34
Artichokes
  Dip, Artichoke and Green
    Chile, 16
  Veal Chops, Artichoke, 106
Asparagus with Mock Hollandaise
  Sauce, 162

Bananas
  Bread, Banana, 40
  Salad, Fresh Fruit, 140
  Spiced Bananas, 44
Beans
  Black
    Dip, Black Bean, 13
    Lasagna Rolls, Black Bean, 87
    Salad Supreme, Taco, 159
    Soup, Black Bean, 182
  Chili, Hearty Sausage-Bean, 191
  Green Beans, Seasoned, 164
  Jambalaya Stew, 184
  Salad, Three-Bean, 148
  Soup, Wagon Wheel Beef, 189
Beef
  Ground
    Meat Loaves, Individual, 97
    Pizza, Mexican, 96
    Soup, Wagon Wheel Beef, 189
  Kabobs, Beef, 99
  Pot Roast, Picante, 104

Steak
  Grilled Flank Steak with Corn
    Salsa, 103
  Stir-Fry, Beef and Pepper, 101
  Stroganoff, Beef, 100
  Tenderloin with Horseradish Sauce,
    Beef, 105
Beverages
  Cider Supreme, Mulled, 20
  Mocha Punch, 24
  Orange-Pineapple Slush, 22
  Punch, Pink Tulip, 23
  Raspberry Tea Spritzer, 21
Biscuits
  Cheddar Drop Biscuits, 28
  Italian Biscuit Knots, 29
Blueberry Muffins, 32
Bran
  Muffins, Applesauce-Bran, 34
  Muffins, Carrot-Pineapple-
    Bran, 35
Breads. *See also* specific types.
  Banana Bread, 40
  Cheese
    Biscuits, Cheddar Drop, 28
    Caraway-Swiss Casserole
      Bread, 42
    Chile-Cheese Cornbread, 36
    French Bread, Cheesy, 27
  Cumin Quick Bread, 38
  Pumpkin Bread, Spiced, 41
  Scones, 30
  Yeast
    Caraway-Swiss Casserole
      Bread, 42
Broccoli
  Casserole, Broccoli-Cheese, 163
  Soup, Chicken Divan, 186
Bulgur
  Tabbouleh, 152

Cabbage
  Coleslaw, Colorful, 146

Cakes
  Cheesecakes
    Chocolate Cheesecake, 50
    Chocolate-Peppermint Ice Cream
      Cake, 60
Carrots
  Muffins, Carrot-Pineapple-Bran, 35
  Orange-Glazed Carrots, 166
Casseroles. *See also* Lasagna.
  Broccoli-Cheese Casserole, 163
  Cordon Bleu Casserole, 124
  Sausage-Egg Casserole, 116
  Squash Casserole, Cheesy, 168
  Wild Rice and Chicken
    Casserole, 119
Cheese. *See also* Appetizers/Cheese.
  Breads
    Biscuits, Cheddar Drop, 28
    Caraway-Swiss Casserole
      Bread, 42
    Cornbread, Chile-Cheese, 36
    French Bread, Cheesy, 27
  Casserole, Broccoli-Cheese, 163
  Casserole, Cheesy Squash, 168
  Casserole, Cordon Bleu, 124
  Chicken, Crispy Cheese-Filled, 128
  Chicken, Ham and Cheese, 127
  Cornbread, Chile-Cheese, 36
  Dip, Swiss-Onion, 15
  Grits, Zippy Garlic-Cheese, 175
  Lasagna Rolls, Black Bean, 87
  Lasagna, Spinach, 85
  Macaroni and Cheese, 177
  Omelets, Potato-Cheddar, 80
  Pie, Vegetable-Cheese, 84
  Sandwiches, Grilled Cheese, 192
Cherries
  Trifle, Black Forest, 49
Chicken
  Cashew Chicken, 123
  Casserole, Cordon Bleu, 124
  Casserole, Wild Rice and
    Chicken, 119
  Cheese-Filled Chicken, Crispy, 128
  Curry, Chicken, 120
  Fajitas, Chicken, 125
  Grilled Firecracker Chicken, 129
  Grilled Lime Chicken, 130

Ham and Cheese Chicken, 127
Mustard Sauce, Chicken in, 131
Pie, Chicken Dumpling, 118
Pockets, Spicy Chicken, 195
Raspberry-Orange Chicken, 133
Salad, Fruited Chicken, 156
Salad, Grilled Chicken Caesar, 157
Sandwiches, Marinated
  Chicken, 196
Soup, Chicken Divan, 186
Soup, Spinach-Chicken Noodle, 187
Strips, Spicy Chicken, 121
Chili, Hearty Sausage-Bean, 191
Chocolate
  Bars, Chocolate Cereal, 48
  Cake, Chocolate-Peppermint Ice
    Cream, 60
  Cheesecake, Chocolate, 50
  Ice Cream, Chocolate, 52
  Ice Cream, Fudgy Peanut Butter, 53
  Trifle, Black Forest, 49
Clams, Steamed, 73
Coffee
  Dessert, Ice Cream Sandwich, 57
  Punch, Mocha, 24
Cookies
  Bars, Chocolate Cereal, 48
Corn
  Salad, Mexican Corn, 149
  Salsa, Grilled Flank Steak with
    Corn, 103
Cornbreads
  Chile-Cheese Cornbread, 36
  Salad, Cornbread, 144
Crab Cakes, Seasoned, 72
Curry
  Chicken Curry, 120
  Shrimp Curry, Light, 77

Desserts. *See also* specific types.
  Chocolate
    Bars, Chocolate Cereal, 48
    Cake, Chocolate-Peppermint Ice
      Cream, 60
    Cheesecake, Chocolate, 50
    Ice Cream, Chocolate, 52
    Ice Cream, Fudgy Peanut Butter, 53
    Trifle, Black Forest, 49

Frozen
    Chocolate Ice Cream, 52
    Chocolate-Peppermint Ice Cream
        Cake, 60
    Cookies 'n Cream Crunch, 58
    Fudgy Peanut Butter Ice Cream, 53
    Ice Cream Sandwich Dessert, 57
    Peach Ice Cream, Homemade, 55
    Pineapple Yogurt with Raspberries,
        Frozen, 56
Fruit
    Bananas, Spiced, 44
    Peach Ice Cream, Homemade, 55
    Pineapple Yogurt with Raspberries,
        Frozen, 56
    Orange-Pumpkin Tarts, 45
    Strawberry Tarts, 47
    Trifle, Black Forest, 49

Eggplant, Italian Stuffed, 93
Eggs
    Casserole, Sausage-Egg, 116
    Frittata, Vegetable, 82
    Omelets
        Potato-Cheddar Omelets, 80
        Spinach-Mushroom Omelet, 81

Fajitas, Chicken, 125
Fish. *See also* Seafood.
    Catfish, Pan-Fried, 62
    Dinner, Hobo Fish, 65
    Flounder, Easy Parmesan, 63
    Grouper, Spicy Grilled, 64
    Orange Roughy, Sesame-Baked, 67
    Red Snapper, Italian, 68
    Salmon on Greens, Grilled, 160
    Salmon, Zesty Baked, 69
    Tuna, Soy-Lime Grilled, 70
French Toast, Cinnamon, 26
Fruit. *See also* specific types.
    Salad, Fresh Fruit, 140
    Salad, Fruited Chicken, 156

Grapefruit and Greens, 142
Grapes
    Salad, Fruited Chicken, 156
Grits, Zippy Garlic-Cheese, 175
Gumbo, Seafood, 190

Ham
    Chicken, Ham and Cheese, 127
    Orange-Baked Ham, 115
    Soup, Black Bean, 182

Ice Creams
    Chocolate Ice Cream, 52
    Cookies 'n Cream Crunch, 58
    Fudgy Peanut Butter Ice Cream, 53
    Peach Ice Cream, Homemade, 55
    Sandwich Dessert, Ice Cream, 57

Jambalaya Stew, 184

Kabobs, Beef, 99

Lamb
    Chops Dijon, Grilled Lamb, 108
    Leg of Lamb, Parslied, 109
Lasagna
    Rolls, Black Bean Lasagna, 87
    Spinach Lasagna, 85
Lemon
    Pasta, Garlic-Lemon, 180
    Shrimp, Lemon-Garlic, 78
Lime
    Chicken, Grilled Lime, 130
    Tuna, Soy-Lime Grilled, 70

Macaroni and Cheese, 177
Melon-Cucumber Salad, 141
Muffins
    Applesauce-Bran Muffins, 34
    Blueberry Muffins, 32
    Carrot-Pineapple-Bran Muffins, 35
Mushrooms
    Kabobs, Beef, 99
    Omelet, Spinach-Mushroom, 81
    Stroganoff, Beef, 100

Noodle Soup, Spinach-Chicken, 187

Okra
    Jambalaya Stew, 184
    Oven-Fried Okra, Crispy, 167
Omelets
    Potato-Cheddar Omelets, 80
    Spinach-Mushroom Omelet, 81

Onion Dip, Swiss-, 15
Oranges
  Carrots, Orange-Glazed, 166
  Chicken, Raspberry-Orange, 133
  Dip, Orange, 14
  Ham, Orange-Baked, 115
  Salad, Fresh Fruit, 140
  Salad, Orange-Pecan Mixed
      Green, 143
  Slush, Orange-Pineapple, 22
  Sweet Potatoes, Orange, 174
  Tarts, Orange-Pumpkin, 45

Pastas. *See also* Lasagna, Macaroni,
    Noodles.
  Garlic-Lemon Pasta, 180
  Linguine with Red Pepper
      Sauce, 179
  Minestrone, 183
  Salad, Garden Pasta, 154
  Scallop and Pasta Toss, 75
  Soup, Wagon Wheel Beef, 189
Peach Ice Cream, Homemade, 55
Peanut Butter Ice Cream, Fudgy, 53
Pears
  Salad, Fresh Fruit, 140
Pecans
  Salad, Orange-Pecan Mixed
      Green, 143
  Waffles, Yogurt-Pecan, 31
Peppers
  Buns, Sausage-Pepper, 197
  Chile
    Cornbread, Chile-Cheese, 36
    Dip, Artichoke and Green
        Chile, 16
  Green
    Kabobs, Beef, 99
    Pizza, Mexican, 96
    Pizza, Three-Pepper, 89
    Stir-Fry, Beef and Pepper, 101
  Pizza, Three-Pepper, 89
  Salad, Jalapeño Potato, 153
  Sauce, Linguine with Red
      Pepper, 179
Pies and Pastries
  Main Dish
    Chicken Dumpling Pie, 118

Vegetable-Cheese Pie, 84
    Vegetable Pot Pie, Roasted, 94
  Tarts
    Orange-Pumpkin Tarts, 45
    Strawberry Tarts, 47
  Vegetable
    Cheese Pie, Vegetable-, 84
    Roasted Vegetable Pot Pie, 94
Pineapple
  Ball, Pineapple Cheese, 18
  Muffins, Carrot-Pineapple-
      Bran, 35
  Salad, Fruited Chicken, 156
  Slush, Orange-Pineapple, 22
  Yogurt with Raspberries, Frozen
      Pineapple, 56
Pizza
  Mexican Pizza, 96
  Pepper Pizza, Three-, 89
  Turkey French Bread Pizzas, 134
Pork. *See also* Ham, Sausage.
  Chops
    Parmesan, Easy Pork, 111
    Skillet-Barbecued Pork Chops, 110
  Peppercorn Pork Loin Roast, 114
  Tenderloin with Cream Sauce,
      Grilled, 113
Potatoes. *See also* Sweet Potatoes.
  Omelets, Potato-Cheddar, 80
  Roasted-Garlic Mashed
      Potatoes, 171
  Roasted New Potatoes, 173
  Salad, Jalapeño Potato, 153
Pumpkin
  Bread, Spiced Pumpkin, 41
  Tarts, Orange-Pumpkin, 45

Raspberries
  Chicken, Raspberry-Orange, 133
  Punch, Pink Tulip, 23
  Spritzer, Raspberry Tea, 21
  Yogurt with Raspberries, Frozen
      Pineapple, 56
Rice
  Casserole, Wild Rice and
      Chicken, 119
  Mexican Rice, Spicy, 176
  Salad, Confetti Rice, 151

Salads
  Bean Salad, Three-, 148
  Chicken Caesar Salad, Grilled, 157
  Chicken Salad, Fruited, 156
  Coleslaw, Colorful, 146
  Cornbread Salad, 144
  Corn Salad, Mexican, 149
  Fruit Salad, Fresh, 140
  Grapefruit and Greens, 142
  Melon-Cucumber Salad, 141
  Orange-Pecan Mixed Green
      Salad, 143
  Pasta Salad, Garden, 154
  Potato Salad, Jalapeño, 153
  Rice Salad, Confetti, 151
  Salmon on Greens, Grilled, 160
  Tabbouleh, 152
  Taco Salad Supreme, 159
Salsa, Speedy, 12
Sandwiches
  Cheese Sandwiches, Grilled, 192
  Chicken Pockets, Spicy, 195
  Chicken Sandwiches,
      Marinated, 196
  Club Sandwiches, 193
  Sausage-Pepper Buns, 197
Sausage
  Buns, Sausage-Pepper, 197
  Casserole, Sausage-Egg, 116
  Chili, Hearty Sausage-Bean, 191
Scallop and Pasta Toss, 75
Seafood. See also Clams, Crab,
      Fish, Scallop, Shrimp.
  Gumbo, Seafood, 190
Shrimp
  Barbecued Shrimp, 76
  Curry, Light Shrimp, 77
  Lemon-Garlic Shrimp, 78
Soups. See also Chili, Gumbo,
      Jambalaya, Stew.
  Bean Soup, Black, 182
  Beef Soup, Wagon Wheel, 189
  Chicken Divan Soup, 186
  Chicken Noodle Soup, Spinach-, 187
  Minestrone, 183
Spinach
  Lasagna, Spinach, 85
  Omelet, Spinach-Mushroom, 81

  Sesame Spinach, Simple, 170
  Soup, Spinach-Chicken Noodle, 187
Squash, Yellow
  Casserole, Cheesy Squash, 168
  Kabobs, Beef, 99
Stew, Jambalaya, 184
Strawberry Tarts, 47
Sweet Potatoes, Orange, 174

Tacos, Seasoned Vegetable, 90
Tomatoes
  Kabobs, Beef, 99
  Red Snapper, Italian, 68
  Salsa, Speedy, 12
Tortillas. See also Fajitas, Tacos.
  Vegetable Burritos, 88
Turkey
  Breast, Roasted Turkey, 138
  Piccata, Turkey, 135
  Pizzas, Turkey French Bread, 134
  Salad Supreme, Taco, 159
  Sandwiches, Club, 193
  Tenderloins, Rosemary Turkey, 137

Veal Chops, Artichoke, 106
Vegetables. See also specific types.
  Burritos, Vegetable, 88
  Chicken Pockets, Spicy, 195
  Frittata, Vegetable, 82
  Minestrone, 183
  Pie, Roasted Vegetable Pot, 94
  Pie, Vegetable-Cheese, 84
  Tacos, Seasoned Vegetable, 90

Waffles, Yogurt-Pecan, 31

Yogurt
  Dip, Orange, 14
  Frozen Pineapple Yogurt with
      Raspberries, 56
  Waffles, Yogurt-Pecan, 31

See page 206 for Quick and Easy Recipe lists.

Quick and Easy Recipes

Ready in 30 Minutes! (or less)

Appetizers and Beverages
Black Bean Dip, 13
Orange Dip, 14
Orange-Pineapple Slush, 22
Pizza Bites, 19
Raspberry Tea Spritzer, 21
Speedy Salsa, 12

Breads
Cheddar Drop Biscuits, 28
Cheesy French Bread, 27
Cinnamon French Toast, 26
Yogurt-Pecan Waffles, 31

Desserts
Spiced Bananas, 44

Fish and Shellfish
Easy Parmesan Flounder, 63
Italian Red Snapper, 68
Pan-Fried Catfish, 62
Scallop and Pasta Toss, 75
Seasoned Crab Cakes, 72
Steamed Clams, 73
Zesty Baked Salmon, 69

Meatless Main Dishes
Seasoned Vegetable Tacos, 90
Three-Pepper Pizza, 89
Vegetable Burritos, 88
Vegetable Frittata, 82

Meats
Beef Kabobs, 99

Poultry
Chicken in Mustard Sauce, 131
Grilled Firecracker Chicken, 129
Turkey French Bread Pizzas, 134
Turkey Piccata, 135

Salads
Fresh Fruit Salad, 140
Grapefruit and Greens, 142
Orange-Pecan Mixed Green
Salad, 143

Sides
Garlic-Lemon Pasta, 180
Orange-Glazed Carrots, 166

Soups
Chicken Divan Soup, 186
Jambalaya Stew, 184

Sandwiches
Club Sandwiches, 193
Grilled Cheese Sandwiches, 192
Sausage-Pepper Buns, 197

Make Ahead!

Salads
Colorful Coleslaw, 146
Confetti Rice Salad, 151
Fruited Chicken Salad, 156
Garden Pasta Salad, 154
Jalapeño Potato Salad, 153
Melon-Cucumber Salad, 141
Mexican Corn Salad, 149
Tabbouleh, 152
Three-Bean Salad, 148

Desserts
Black Forest Trifle, 49
Chocolate Cereal Bars, 48
Chocolate-Peppermint Ice Cream
Cake, 60
Cookies 'n Cream Crunch, 58

Metric Equivalents

The recipes that appear in this cookbook use the standard United States method for measuring liquid and dry or solid ingredients (teaspoons, tablespoons, and cups). The information in the following charts is provided to help cooks outside the U.S. successfully use these recipes. All equivalents are approximate.

Equivalents for Different Types of Ingredients

A standard cup measure of a dry or solid ingredient will vary in weight depending on the type of ingredient. A standard cup of liquid is the same volume for any type of liquid. Use the following chart when converting standard cup measures to grams (weight) or milliliters (volume).

Standard Cup	Fine Powder (ex. flour)	Grain (ex. rice)	Granular (ex. sugar)	Liquid Solids (ex. butter)	Liquid (ex. milk)
1	140 g	150 g	190 g	200 g	240 ml
¾	105 g	113 g	143 g	150 g	180 ml
⅔	93 g	100 g	125 g	133 g	160 ml
½	70 g	75 g	95 g	100 g	120 ml
⅓	47 g	50 g	63 g	67 g	80 ml
¼	35 g	38 g	48 g	50 g	60 ml
⅛	18 g	19 g	24 g	25 g	30 ml

Dry Ingredients by Weight

(To convert ounces to grams, multiply the number of ounces by 30.)

1 oz	=	¹⁄₁₆ lb	=	30 g
4 oz	=	¼ lb	=	120 g
8 oz	=	½ lb	=	240 g
12 oz	=	¾ lb	=	360 g
16 oz	=	1 lb	=	480 g

Length

(To convert inches to centimeters, multiply the number of inches by 2.5.)

1 in	=			=	2.5 cm	
6 in	=	½ ft		=	15 cm	
12 in	=	1 ft		=	30 cm	
36 in	=	3 ft	= 1 yd	=	90 cm	
40 in	=			=	100 cm	= 1 m

Liquid Ingredients by Volume

¼ tsp							1 ml	
½ tsp							2 ml	
1 tsp							5 ml	
3 tsp	=	1 tbls		=	½ fl oz	=	15 ml	
		2 tbls	= ⅛ cup	=	1 fl oz	=	30 ml	
		4 tbls	= ¼ cup	=	2 fl oz	=	60 ml	
		5⅓ tbls	= ⅓ cup	=	3 fl oz	=	80 ml	
		8 tbls	= ½ cup	=	4 fl oz	=	120 ml	
		10⅔ tbls	= ⅔ cup	=	5 fl oz	=	160 ml	
		12 tbls	= ¾ cup	=	6 fl oz	=	180 ml	
		16 tbls	= 1 cup	=	8 fl oz	=	240 ml	
		1 pt	= 2 cups	=	16 fl oz	=	480 ml	
		1 qt	= 4 cups	=	32 fl oz	=	960 ml	
					33 fl oz	=	1000 ml	= 1 liter

Cooking/Oven Temperatures

	Fahrenheit	Celsius	Gas Mark
Freeze Water	32° F	0° C	
Room Temperature	68° F	20° C	
Boil Water	212° F	100° C	
Bake	325° F	160° C	3
	350° F	180° C	4
	375° F	190° C	5
	400° F	200° C	6
	425° F	220° C	7
	450° F	230° C	8
Broil			Grill